STORIES
OF OUR PAST

LOUISBOURG

Past, Present, Future

DISCARD

A. J. B. Johnston

NIMBUS
PUBLISHING

Nimbus Publishing Limited
3731 Mackintosh St, Halifax, NS B3K 5A5
(902) 455-4286 nimbus.ca

Printed and bound in Canada

Author photo: Chris Reardon
Interior and cover design: Jenn Embree
Cover image: Ian Harte
NB 1061

Library and Archives Canada Cataloguing in Publication

Johnston, A. J. B.
Louisbourg : past, present, future / A. J. B. Johnston.
Includes bibliographical references and index.
Issued also in an electronic format.
ISBN 978-1-77108-052-1

1. Louisbourg (N.S.)—History. I. Title.

FC2349.L6J645 2013   971.6'955   C2012-907385-7

Nimbus Publishing acknowledges the financial support for its publishing activities from the Government of Canada through the Canada Book Fund (CBF) and the Canada Council for the Arts, and from the Province of Nova Scotia through the Department of Communities, Culture and Heritage.

MIX
Paper from responsible sources
FSC
www.fsc.org   FSC® C103113

For Louisbourg's many unsung heroes, from archivists and artisans, to carpenters and clerks, to seamstresses, soldiers, and stonemasons, without whose countless contributions we wouldn't have the place at all, not once but twice, two centuries apart.

ACKNOWLEDGEMENTS

The idea for this book came from Patrick Murphy, managing editor of Nimbus Publishing. He suggested, in a May 2012 conversation with A. J. B. (John) Johnston, that it might be appropriate to have a new book on Louisbourg to mark the tercentenary of the French founding in 1713. John mulled it over for a couple of days and decided that yes, Patrick was right, and that such a book should seek to tell the Louisbourg story in a more sweeping way than it has ever been told before. That would mean beginning the history five thousand years ago—when the harbour was formed—and continuing on through the French period, the nineteenth and twentieth centuries, and into the likely near future. *Louisbourg: Past, Present, Future* is the result.

Right from the start, John wanted to enlist Parks Canada historian Anne Marie Lane Jonah and Parks Canada archaeologist Rebecca Dunham as contributors to the project. The short essays they wrote specifically for the book add an extra dimension that gives the text much-needed depth in what are but a few areas of their expertise. Thanks to both Becki and Anne Marie for their contributions.

Key players at the review and production phase were editor Whitney Moran and designer Jenn Embree of Nimbus Publishing. Many thanks to both.

CONTENTS

A striking image of today's Fortress of Louisbourg.

THE HARBOUR BEFORE 1713

Havre à l'Anglois

English Harbour

Port Inglese

MOST VISITORS these days find Louisbourg at the end of Route 22. It's usually a half hour drive from Sydney or half a day from Halifax or Truro on the Nova Scotia mainland. How different it was in times gone by. In the centuries before the advent of the automobile, the people who came to Louisbourg—and there were many thousands who came to live, do business there, or wage war—almost always arrived by sea. For in that bygone era, the oceans were the world's highways, and mariners from seagoing countries plied the waters of the globe the way today's travellers and goods go up and down by air. Yes, it took much longer than it does now, but it was the fastest way there was— and in many situations, the only choice. And, yes, there were incredible perils of shipboard sicknesses, storms at sea, and the occasional shipwreck with all lives lost. Nonetheless, the possible rewards of reaching Louisbourg—better lives, profits to be made, or a colony to be defended or attacked—outweighed the risks many times to one.

Two and a half to three centuries ago, vessels, once safely through Louisbourg's narrow harbour entrance—having sailed past one of only two lighthouses in all of North America at the time—moved into the encircling harbour that was the destination of the trip. That harbour always contained many ships

The scale of the reconstruction at Louisbourg is impressive, without any doubt. Yet, what is rebuilt is but one-fifth of the original walled town.

and boats regardless of the time of year, though the spring-to-fall shipping season was far busier than the winter, when it was local traffic only. Let's imagine that one of the people arriving is of a reflective nature; he or she cannot help but admire and wonder about the town and seaport before his or her eyes. How is it that there is a fully developed French town with 250 or so buildings within Vauban-style fortification walls on the edge of this otherwise unpopulated shoreline of the New World? Who lives in this place and why; what will its future be?

Those imagined questions are precisely the ones we seek to answer in this book—not once but twice. That's because the story of Louisbourg as a fortified French town begins in the eighteenth century then reappears in the twentieth century. The latter was (and still is) an ambitious attempt to educate the public about its predecessor's storied past.

Costumed animators bring eighteenth-century Louisbourg back to life—most magically of all in special events held after dark.

Before we launch into the details of the human drama of the "two Louisbourgs," however, it is vitally important to say something about the harbour they share, and about the adjacent sea. That harbour and the maritime world beyond were the single most important factors in French colonial Louisbourg's growth into a major fishing and commercial seaport and military stronghold. (We explain why in the chapters to come.) The point we want to make right now is that the harbour and the sea that feeds it are not fixed. They have always been what they are now: dynamic.

Over time, sea levels and the very earth upon which we stand expand and contract and move up and down. In the specific case of Louisbourg, such natural forces created the conditions for the settlement to become what it was for the French. Those same natural forces are still very much in play, only now they are causing serious erosion and threatening to eventually flood portions of the twentieth-century reconstruction of the eighteenth-century town.

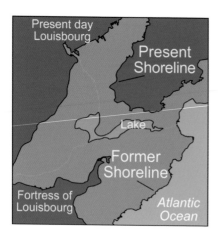

Present day Louisbourg

Present Shoreline

Lake

Former Shoreline

Fortress of Louisbourg

Atlantic Ocean

This map, developed by the Geological Survey of Canada in the 1990s, shows the situation at Louisbourg more than five thousand years ago. Until the sea level rose enough, there was no harbour, only a lake.

If we were to go back 11,500 years, the sea level off Nova Scotia's eastern shore was approximately sixty-five metres (213.25 feet) below where it stands today. The ocean continued to rise in the millennia that followed, both because the Earth's climate was generally warming (though there was a long period during which it was not), and because of the effect of crustal subsidence. Still, it took a long time to get to where we are today. Nine thousand years ago, Halifax's Bedford Basin was an inland lake. There was still no Northumberland Strait, meaning that Prince Edward Island was attached to the mainland of Canada. As for Louisbourg, it was not until about five thousand years ago that the salt water from the Atlantic rose high enough to flood what, until then, had been an inland lake. A kidney-shaped harbour slowly formed.

As the coast continued to submerge and the glaciers melted, the seawater continued to rise. How frequently the Mi'kmaq might have been to that part of the Cape Breton coastline over the span of a few thousand years is unknown. But we do know—from an account of an English sailing voyage in 1593—that by that date the seasonal round of some Mi'kmaq definitely included Louisbourg. The ship on that particular voyage was the *Marigold*.

Captained by Richard Strong, the primary purpose of the

Crustal Subsidence and Sea Level Rise

1744, 1759 plans & 1989 aerial
East side of fortress
(not reconstructed)

Up until about ten thousand years ago, and for roughly one hundred thousand years previously, there were vast ice sheets, several kilometres high, across much of the northern hemisphere. When the glaciers melted (as they are continuing to do where they still exist) the meltwater causes the level of the world's oceans to rise. At Louisbourg, that has meant an average sea level rise of 1.6 millimetres per year.

Quite apart from that phenomenon is the fact that, throughout much of Atlantic Canada, there are coastal areas submerging independently of rising water levels caused by melting glaciers and thermal expansion. (Thermal expansion is the phenomenon of materials and liquids increasing in volume as they heat up.) Measurements taken along the Atlantic coast of Nova Scotia since 1920 have documented an annual average crustal subsidence of 1.6 millimetres per year. When combined, the separate forces produce an annual 3.2-millimetre relative increase in sea level. Multiply that figure by a decade or a century and you will quickly grasp the issue. Humans have contributed to the process over the last few centuries by steadily burning more fossil fuels; while this is not the underlying cause of relative sea level rise, it has nonetheless sped up the clock.

Marigold's trans-Atlantic voyage was to hunt walruses on the Magdalen Islands; but it continued on to Cape Breton, where the crew hauled in a great many lobsters at Cibou (Sydney) and saw a large number of seals closer to Louisbourg. Sailing into what, after 1713, would be called Louisbourg, the English crew went ashore to obtain fresh water. To the European mariners of the time, the haven had various names: "Port Inglese," "English Port," and "Havre à l'Anglois," all of which suggest either the

The Mi'kmaq and Early Contact with the French

The historical consensus is that before the arrival of Europeans, the Mi'kmaq of Unama'ki (the Mi'kmaw name for Cape Breton Island) were primarily focussed on the Bras d'Or Lake. However, different bands certainly did travel to coastal areas in the summer months to harvest seasonal resources and, after the arrival of the Europeans, to trade. In the mid-1600s, when Nicolas Denys had small French colonies at Sainte-Anne (Englishtown) and Saint-Pierre (today's St. Peter's), these two posts were places of frequent contact between the French and the Mi'kmaq.

regular use of the anchorage by the English, or that they were the first to put its name on a map.

The author of the *Marigold*'s journal, one Richard Fisher, reported finding raspberries, strawberries, and sweet-smelling herbs, as well as "goodly" oaks, fir trees of "great height," and "quickbeams" (a type of mountain ash) at the future Louisbourg. The English also encountered the Mi'kmaq. Fisher says the Aboriginal peoples had fish pens there as well as weirs. Initially, the Mi'kmaq greeted the English in a friendly way, until the newcomers fired their muskets. At that point, the Mi'kmaq took up staves to defend their lives, as well as their use of the area.

In 1597, four years later, another English ship, the *Hopewell*, under a Captain Charles Leigh, left an account of another voyage into Cape Breton waters. This time the writer makes only a passing mention of the "English Port" (Louisbourg), and no mention at all of Mi'kmaq. Perhaps the increasing use of the anchorage by Europeans during the summer months had convinced the Mi'kmaq to go elsewhere for the resources they used to harvest at Louisbourg. That seems a reasonable conclusion, because Capt. Leigh's voyage makes it clear that the coastline of eastern Cape Breton was bustling with European ships and sailors in 1597. At New Port (Baleine), just up the coast from Louisbourg, there was even an "admiral." This was the title given to the first ship's captain to arrive each season, whose duty and honour it was to regulate disputes and deliver a basic system of justice among the different captains and crews who would be fishing and trading along the coast that summer.

The next intriguing glimpse of activity at Louisbourg comes from the quill of colonizer and writer Nicolas Denys. He provided a short description of Louisbourg harbour in his justly renowned book on the fishery, *Description géographique et historique des costes de l'Amérique sep-*

DESCRIPTION
GEOGRAPHIQUE
ET HISTORIQUE
DES COSTES
DE L'AMERIQVE
SEPTENTRIONALE.
Avec l'Hiftoire naturelle du Païs.
*Par Monfieur DENYS, Gouverneur Lieutenant
General pour le Roy, & proprietaire de toutes
les Terres & Ifles qui font depuis le Cap de
Campfeaux, jufques au Cap des Roziers.*
TOME I.

A PARIS,
Chez CLAUDE BARBIN, au Palais,
fur le Perron de la fainte Chapelle.

M. DC. LXXII.
Avec Privilege du Roy.

For more than three centuries, historians and anthropologists have been mining Nicolas Denys's writings to see what he had to say about the fisheries, the Mi'kmaq, and the natural history of the Maritimes.

tentrionale: avec l'histoire naturelle du païs, or in English, *The description and natural history of the coasts of North America [Acadia]*. Denys describes it as being a "good" anchorage, and states that there is a "pond where are caught great numbers of Eels. The fishery for Cod is very good there. The men of Olonne came here in old times to winter in order to be first upon the Grand Banc for the fishery of green Cod, and to be first back to France, because the fish is sold much better when first brought in."

There are two aspects of importance in that short description. The first is that it establishes eels at Louisbourg. Eels were

This view, painted by a French engineer known as Verrier *fils*, was drawn in 1731. It depicts Louisbourg as it was less than two decades after its founding. The engineer in charge of the construction at Louisbourg between 1724 and 1745 was Étienne Verrier. Verrier *fils* refers to his son, Claude-Étienne Verrier.

an important part of the diet of the Mi'kmaq, so it was likely eels they were fishing for in the ponds described in the 1593 *Marigold* account. The second aspect is the reference to the "men of Olonne" overwintering at Louisbourg "in old times." Denys is referring to the fishermen from Les Sables d'Olonne, a town situated slightly to the north of La Rochelle on the west coast of France. From these few words, we can deduce that those fishers must have constructed shelters (and presumably wharves and other rudimentary structures associated with the green fishery) at Louisbourg at some point prior to the 1650s. When Denys writes "in old times," it is difficult to know if he is referring to the early 1600s or the late 1500s. Whatever the period—and who knows how long the practice lasted—the first temporary French occupation of the future Louisbourg appears to have been by fishers from Les Sables d'Olonne.

The era of private fishing and trading ventures sailing out of French, English, Portuguese, Spanish, and Basque ports and into Cape Breton's waters and anchorages lasted for a couple hundred years, without any kind of effective "state" control or order. Beginning in 1713, however, that long period was about to come to an end. The stakes in the next phase, which was one of greatly intensified imperial conflict between Great Britain and France, would be high on all sides. Louisbourg, once founded, would be front and centre in that new era.

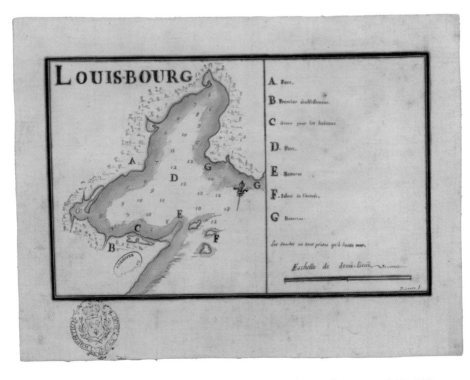

In this plan, drawn soon after the founding of Louisbourg in 1713, "A" indicates an early fort, "B" is where people first settled, "C" is a shoreline for fishing properties, and "E" and "G" are gun batteries.

CHAPTER 1

AN ASPIRATION BECOMES A REALITY

Port Saint-Louis

Louisbourg

IN THE late 1500s and throughout the 1600s, the anchorage that would become Louisbourg harbour was far from unknown and unused. Yet it would not be until the waning days of the summer of 1713 that a town—meaning year-round residents living in permanent buildings—began to rise on its shores. But before we say more about that founding, we should provide a little background on how and why it took place when it did.

Prior to the 1713 establishment of Louisbourg and other smaller French settlements on Île Royale (Cape Breton Island), colonial ventures in Atlantic Canada had been relatively small and weakly supported by the French crown. Acadia (mainland Nova Scotia) began on a tiny scale, with dozens of men but no women or children. During the first half of the 1600s, private companies were taking the lead. Families from France started arriving in Acadia in the 1630s, and it took another thirty years before the French state became greatly involved.

It was during the reign of Louis XIV that France took over the direct administration of its colonies. It sent officials and soldiers to Canada (Quebec) and Acadia from the 1660s onward, as well as to another Atlantic colony: a major fishing base at Placentia, Newfoundland. None of those ventures, however, enjoyed the kind of backing from France that Louisbourg would later have.

Why Were There Colonies At All?

Reduced to their basics, all European overseas colonies were about economics. Government expenditures were seen as investments in current or future returns. Yes, there was a desire to explore unknown lands and waters, and there was often missionary activity among the Aboriginal peoples, but those initiatives were undertaken to reinforce or supplement the dominant economic and military aims of the colonizer. In the Atlantic region, the cod fishery was by far the economic engine. It provided jobs for thousands of fishers from France, significant profits for investors in port cities, and it was a "nursery of seamen" when wars occurred, which they often did. In the 1760s, after Louisbourg was lost to the British, no less a writer than Voltaire wrote that it had been "the key" to French possessions in North America. "The cod fishery carried out in its waters was the object of a useful commerce, employing each year more than 500 small vessels…. It was a school of sailors; and of commerce; which joined to that of the cod fishery, kept 10,000 men working and circulated 10 millions livres."

France's thinking about its overseas possessions changed dramatically as the end of the War of the Spanish Succession (1701–13) approached. The war had not gone well for the king's armies and navies. Louis XIV was facing the likelihood of handing over sovereignty to Great Britain for a wide swath of territory in North America, including Acadia and Placentia. France faced a choice: either give up some of the areas they had colonized in Atlantic Canada, or establish their presence and back it up with more military force than they had shown before. They chose the latter path. A heavily invested Louisbourg would be the result.

By the terms of the 1713 Treaty of Utrecht, the only possessions remaining under French jurisdiction in the Atlantic region were Île Royale and Île Saint-Jean (Prince Edward Island). France's choice was definitively for Cape Breton. Two memoirs, both written in 1706, had already urged that Cape Breton be settled and developed for a combination of economic and strategic reasons. This small extract from one of the memoirs sums up the argument for a strong economic and strategic presence on the island.

> The proposed settlement brings together all the fisheries under French control, absolutely excludes the English from the same, defends the colonies of Canada, Newfoundland and Acadia from all their efforts, prevents them from making themselves the masters of all these great countries and thus of all the fisheries, ruins the colony of Boston by excluding them from the same without making war on them, it is the refuge of disabled vessels which frequent these seas…it becomes the rendezvous and storehouse of vessels from the Indies, the Islands of America and New Spain, it increases the number of seamen, facilitates the Canada trade…it augments His Majesty's domination and the commerce of his subjects…this is enough to show that this settlement has, in a word, become of indispensable necessity, and that it is time to set ourselves effectively to the task.

The so-called "Sun King" (Roi-Soleil), Louis XIV (1638–1715), ruled France for seventy-two years. Louisbourg was founded in 1713, two years before his death.

In the summer of 1713, with the peace treaty and related territorial loss for France coming into effect, French royal authorities ordered a colonizing mission for Cape Breton Island. They would sail from Placentia, Newfoundland, aboard a ship called the *Semslack*. The mandate was to cruise Île Royale to find the anchorage that, in the minister's words, was "the most suitable for establishing the fort and the most convenient for fishing and commerce." Aboard were a good many fishers who were hoping

The colony of Île Royale was France's latest colony, coming a little more than a century after the beginning of Acadia. The small inset maps show the three harbours in contention to become the main French settlement on the island. Sainte-Anne (Englishtown), Saint-Pierre (St. Peter's), and Louisbourg.

to start over in a place where the cod-fishing was said to be as good as it had been off Newfoundland. The second part of the plan was to attract large numbers of Acadians to Île Royale from their (mostly) farming communities on mainland Nova Scotia. That second hope met with only limited success.

The founding expedition for Île Royale concentrated on the anchorages along the rocky eastern shore. The region held little

Coffee and Tea

Though these two beverages are entirely commonplace today, they were relatively new to Europeans at the time of French colonial Louisbourg. Coffee arrived first, brought into Europe from the Middle East. It spread rapidly and was quite a common drink by the time Louisbourg was founded. Of the 144 household inventories available for study at Louisbourg, 53—from both rich and poor—include coffee and/or a coffee pot. Tea, on the other hand, was a rare drink for the French in the eighteenth century. The French had a small presence in India, at Pondicherry, but drinking tea was seen as supporting the colonial trade of France's enemy, the British. Only two Louisbourg inventories had tea: a governor's and an innkeeper's.
–Anne Marie Lane Jonah

promise for agriculture, but then, it wasn't farmland the mission was looking to find—it sought good harbours that were close to inshore and offshore banks of cod. Once dried, cod was a staple of European diets and a source of wealth as an object of intercolonial and international trade. After much more than a century's experience fishing off Cape Breton, the French knew exactly where the cod were to be found, and where the sheltered anchorages were along that same stretch of coast.

Besides Havre à l'Anglois (Louisbourg), the 1713 *Semslack* expedition assessed both Sainte-Anne (Englishtown) and Saint-Pierre (St. Peter's), where Nicolas Denys had had fur-trading and fishing ventures a half century before. They found traces of both old posts. The French newcomers also met some of the Mi'kmaq while they were sailing around. According to the leader of the French expedition, Cape Breton Island's population in the summer of 1713 was twenty-five or thirty families of Mi'kmaq and a single Frenchman. Aboard the *Semslack*, relocating from Placentia, was a civilian population of 116 men, 10 women and 23 children, and 100 soldiers originally from France.

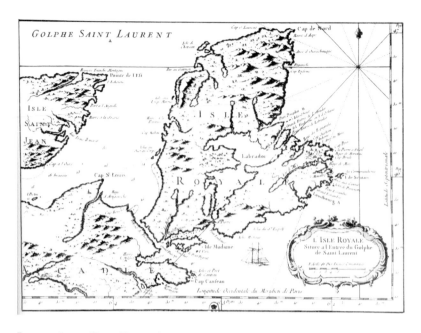

It was along Cape Breton's eastern coastline where most of the French settled during the Louisbourg era.

The leadership of the expedition knew that summer would not last forever. A harbour had to be selected while there was still time to erect shelters, cut firewood, and generally prepare for the onset of winter. The fishing population would need to build wharves and flakes, prepare cobbled beaches, and get boats and nets ready. There was, at the time, a winter fishing season, and no one wanted to miss out.

The fishers made it clear which anchorage they preferred, and the expedition's leadership agreed. So it was that on September 2, 1713, Havre à l'Anglois was selected as the principal settlement of France's latest colony. At the time, the "royal" name for the island was only an aspiration. However, over the next forty-five years, Île Royale—and Louisbourg in particular—would receive unprecedented support and financing from the king, and from the budgets administered by the minister of the marine. There would be impressive fortifications, steadily growing numbers of soldiers, judicial courts, religious orders, a hospital, street plans, public wharves, a lighthouse, and a careening facility where ships could be turned on their sides and have their hulls cleaned and repaired. Such structures and measures required a willingness on the part of French royal authorities to spend substantial sums of money.

Lewis Parker's 1980s sketch depicts the careening wharf already in existence, in the foreground, while the lighthouse is under construction in the background.

An eighteenth-century Jesuit historian named Charlevoix wrote that the anchorage selected in 1713 was "one of the finest

La Prise de Possession

A formal document was prepared to mark the official "taking of possession" of Louisbourg on September 2, 1713. If a town could have a birth certificate, this was it: a straightforward, succinct recording of what happened. There is no mention of a cross being raised, of a *Te Deum* being sung or even a routine prayer from the priest on board the *Semslack*, or of artillery salutes from the ship. One imagines there must have been a speech or two—but maybe not. After all, there was so much work to be done. The single-page document states what happened in the fewest words possible, and who was there: a few military officers, the engineer, and a priest. All signed the end of the document.

The Cost of Île Royale

By the time Louisbourg and Île Royale fell definitively to the British in 1758, the French kings (first Louis XIV and then Louis XV) had spent about twenty million livres on the colony, four million of which went toward fortifications. It was a huge outlay for the time. During the 1720s, about 10 per cent of all French spending on colonies anywhere was expended at Louisbourg. In the 1730s and 1740s, that share rose to around 20 per cent and above. This financial commitment underlines the importance French colonial authorities attached to Louisbourg and Île Royale. And the expenditures were not in vain. The colony made many people a lot of money. Over the same 1713–58 span, the cod fishery at Île Royale by itself, not counting commerce, returned three or four times the 20 million-livres figure to France.

harbours in all America…the anchorage is good, and ships can be beached without risk. Its entrance is only two hundred fathoms wide, between two small islands, which can easily defend it. The cod fishery is very abundant." What more could someone involved in the fishery—or a royal official, for that matter—ask?

The name initially bestowed on the former Havre à l'Anglois was Port Saint-Louis, a name that honoured the memory of France's cherished thirteenth-century king, Louis IX, who had been canonized. That first choice, however, was quickly changed in France. A secular spirit was in the ascendant—quite different from the piousness that had dominated the state's thinking a century before. Where religious place names had once been very much in vogue, they would not be on Île Royale. So instead of naming this new fishing base and important seaport after a

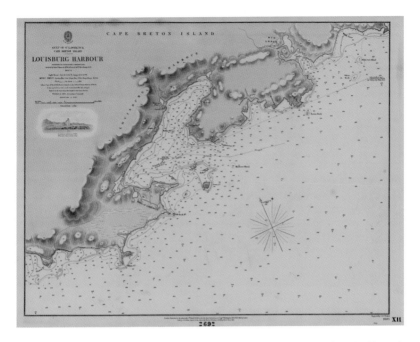

This is an 1857 plan of Louisbourg harbour. That's a century after the French were forced to leave in 1758, yet the kidney-shaped harbour was still much used by mariners of Cape Breton Island.

bygone saint, royal officials decided that it should honour the current king, Louis XIV. The name selected was "Louisbourg." As it turned out, Louis XIV was to die two years later, succeeded by his great-grandson, Louis XV.

From the start, Louisbourg showed itself to have been the right choice, at least for those who fished. The initial 150 civilian settlers soon doubled to more than 300 when additional fishing crews arrived from Placentia. Fishing began right away, and the catches were as good as they had been in Newfoundland. One contemporary English writer quipped that the French were delighted with the new fishing base, saying "ye English gave them a wedge of gold for a piece of silver." Port activity increased to the

This is an archaeological excavation of one of the French fishing properties along Louisbourg harbour. Because of shoreline erosion, the property is now much closer to the waterline than it was two and a half centuries ago.

point that, in 1716, a visiting French ship captain named Louis Chancel de Lagrange described Louisbourg as "the real seat of commerce," and stated, "All the Breton, Basque, Provençal, Olonne and even English merchant vessels put in there."

Some of the military officers and engineers, however, did *not* think Louisbourg a good choice. Excellent for the fishery it may have been, but their concern lay in defending the place should an enemy—most likely the British—ever attack. Louisbourg was situated on low-lying ground that would be difficult and expensive to fortify. These officers worried that an enemy might take advantage of the nearby hills with their cannons, and bombard the town. For a few years, the advice of the engineers and military officers prevailed. The official capital of Île Royale, with the leading royal officials, was not at Louisbourg but at the more

Louis XV (1710–1774) succeeded the French throne at age five, when his great-grandfather, Louis XIV, passed away. Because he was a child, there was a Regency period until 1723, when Louis XV came of age.

This map identifies most of the French settlements on Cape Breton Island during the Louisbourg period.

easily defended Port Dauphin (what had been Sainte-Anne, and today is Englishtown).

Alas for the military point of view, the fishers and traders who preferred Louisbourg stayed where they were. Moreover, others from France, Acadia, and Canada joined them there. Most of the newcomers were men, but there were women and sometimes families as well. They were coming for what they believed would be economic advancement, a phenomenon as old as human history itself, and they were not only fishermen and merchants; there were carpenters and stonemasons, bakers and butchers, seamstresses and servants. Louisbourg was, beyond doubt, the growth centre of Île Royale.

Acadians and Île Royale

With the signing of the Treaty of Utrecht in 1713, French *Acadie* became British Nova Scotia. But people—in this case the *Acadiens* (Acadians)—do not change so quickly. The French-speaking Roman Catholic colonists living in agricultural communities on the shores of the Bay of Fundy and in scattered fishing villages on the Atlantic coast had developed a distinct and thriving society over several generations. They had survived previous British occupations with relatively little impact on their way of life. So only a few carpenters and coastal traders found any appeal in the French king's inducements to relocate to the new colony of Île Royale when it was created in 1713. Farmers were not tempted to leave their fertile farms and take up fishing. Thus through the years that Louisbourg grew, most Acadians stayed in what was now Nova Scotia. Those who did relocate to Île Royale preferred Port Toulouse (today's St. Peter's).

Nonetheless, Louisbourg had a small but important Acadian presence. Some Acadian girls came, married, and raised families. Other Acadians worked in the trades or came and went as traders and shippers, bringing the French settlement valuable produce. Throughout all the communication, or so it appears, the Acadians never forgot their identity. They were *Acadien*, while most of the population of Louisbourg was *Français*. –*Anne Marie Lane Jonah*

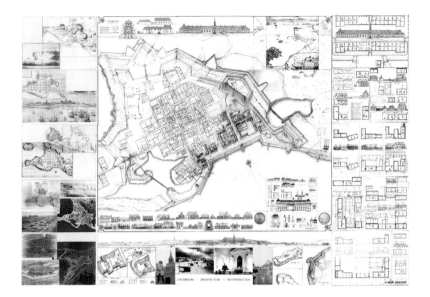

This marvellous drawing by Yvon LeBlanc, who was the restoration architect at the Fortress of Louisbourg National Historic Site from 1972 to 1983, depicts every building within the walls at Louisbourg, circa 1744. The portion that has been coloured in is that which has been reconstructed, in contrast to the more ghost-like remaining four fifths.

The royal administration soon gave up on Port Dauphin and returned to Louisbourg: economics trumped military concerns. The town and its harbour would simply have to be defended at greater cost than other, more easily defended posts. The first fortification sketch dates from 1717. Over the years to come, that initial, simple concept would be greatly altered and enhanced so much that by the 1740s, the town boasted some of the most elaborate fortifications in North America. (We have more to say about that in the next chapter.)

We close this chapter on the ceremonial side of Louisbourg. Life in eighteenth-century European societies was often extremely formal. Monarchies and churches, along with guilds

The King's Bastion stood atop the highest hill on the low-lying peninsula where Louisbourg was built. The multi-purpose building was home to the soldiers' barracks, the governor's apartment, a chapel, a prison, and other functions.

and other institutions, regularly used special occasions to promote and consolidate their roles in society. Louisbourg in 1720 witnessed just such an event. Medals specially struck in a French mint were sent to Louisbourg to mark its founding. They were to be placed in the foundations of the most important public buildings—those paid for by the royal purse. Perhaps you're thinking: but the town was founded in 1713, was it not? Yes it was, but nothing formal had been done to mark the extremely hasty founding of the settlements at that time. So, in 1720, the royal administration in France—during the regency of young Louis XV—ordered the colonial governor to mark with appropriate ceremonies the burial of a number of "Louisbourg foundation" medals. The first location was the King's Bastion area, where

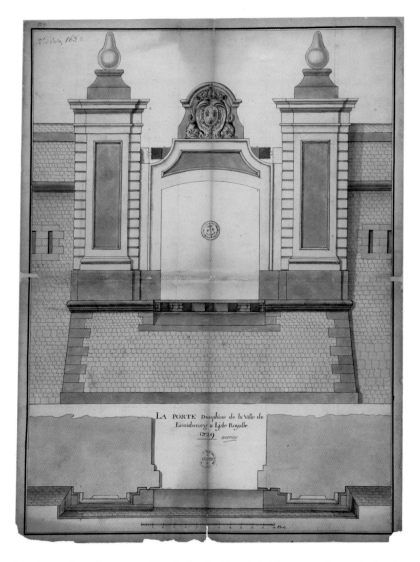

LA PORTE Dauphine de la Ville de
Louisbourg a L'isle Royalle
1729

The Porte Dauphine or, in English, the Dauphin Gate, was the main landward entrance to the fortified town of Louisbourg. This feature has been
reconstructed, and is where soldiers challenge most visitors before they enter
the fortress.

1720 Louisbourg Foundation Medals

In 1962, during the early years of the Louisbourg reconstruction project, archaeological excavation of the right-shoulder angle of the King's Bastion revealed a surprising find. Although this corner of the bastion had been soundly demolished by the British in 1760, archaeologists discovered a small commemoration box tucked inside the interior angle of the right-shoulder wall. Amidst the soil and rubble lay a lead casket, about the size of a large brick (10" x 4 1/2" x 2 1/2"). Enclosed within was a wooden box containing three medals struck to commemorate the construction of the fortress in 1720.

The lead casket had been bolted together and encased a block of white pine with three countersunk holes for placement of the medals. A silver medal was placed in the centre of the block, flanked by two medals of copper alloy. The medals bore the same inscription (LUDOVICUS XV. DG.FFR.ET NAV. REX, which translates to "Louis XV, by Grace of God King of France and Navarre,"), a bust of Louis XV on the obverse, and a scene of the projected fortress and harbour on the reverse with the legend "LUDOVICOBURGUM FUNDATUM ET MUNITUM M.DCC.XX" ("Louisbourg Founded and Fortified 1720"). At the base of Louis XV's bust, the designer signed his work as L.LE. BLANC.F. Once the medals were in place, the wooden block was capped with pine slats, secured to the lead cover with nails and washers, and then placed in the wall, presumably with much pomp and ceremony.

The conserved box and replica medals are currently on display at the Fortress of Louisbourg archaeology office. These are some of the most valued objects in the Louisbourg archaeology collection, for they celebrate not only the beginning of Louisbourg but its reconstruction as well. –*Rebecca Dunham*

the fortifications were just beginning to rise. There would be additional medals buried, and many royal ceremonies of other kinds held, at Louisbourg in the years to come.

A *L'Eglise ou toutes les principales habitations.*
B *Ancient corps de Casernes.*
C *Nouvaux corps de Casernes.*
D *Jardins ou doivent être les edifications.*
E *Bassin de Carene.*
F *Chafoul pour preparer les Morüe;*

Veue du Port de Louis-bourg dans L'Isle Royalle.

G *Chaloupe qui se revient qui vont à la pesche;*
H *Chaloupe qui reviennent de la Pesche;*
I *Grave ou l'on fait sécher la Morüe;*
L *Vigneau ou l'on fait sécher la Morüe.*
M *Pûtre ou Estran pour les grosses de la peche;*
N *Rade ouverte de deux poils et trois a haute Me.*

Louisbourg was the busiest port in New France, and one of the busiest in all of colonial North America. This view is undated and unsigned, but it was likely painted by an engineer (possibly Jean François de Verville) about 1717. This image was almost certainly what was used by the artist who came up with an image of Louisbourg for the reverse of the 1720 foundation medal.

CHAPTER 2

POPULATION, FORTIFICATIONS, GOVERNMENT, AND RELIGION

Dunkirk of North America

Gibraltar of the New World

WITH LOUISBOURG confirmed as the capital of Île Royale in 1720, the settlement was now to enjoy over two decades of peace before war would come to it for the first time. The attack, when it came, would bring great upheaval; but of course no one living through the 1720s, 1730s, or early 1740s knew what lay ahead. They simply went on with their lives the way people do, at work and at leisure. The community at Louisbourg grew at a remarkable pace during this long period of peace.

Census data for Louisbourg exists for a number of years. The authorities gathered information on the population for a variety of reasons, just like governments do today. For instance, when it came to boys, census takers asked how many were under or over age twelve, because this was the age at which males were considered able to fire a musket. In other words, boys twelve and up could serve in the local militia. No such age distinction was made for girls. Females were either girls, women, or widows.

The Government of Île Royale

The time period during which Louisbourg flourished was one when Europeans generally believed that societies were held together by forces and influences emigrating from the top down. At the pinnacle of society—best imagined as a giant social pyramid—was the monarch. Then came the upper clergy and nobles, down to countless lower levels where less influential people carefully guarded their places in the overall scheme of things. Specifically at Louisbourg, the governor represented the king. He was answerable to senior officials in France, yet he also had to share power and authority on Île Royale with another appointed royal official: the financial administrator (*commissaire-ordonnateur*).

It was very much a check-and-balance approach to government, with some overlapping jurisdictions, detailed codes and regulations, and one official keeping an eye on the other. Over time, Louisbourg was home to a higher and lower civil and criminal court system and a maritime court as well. The three courts handled routine regulatory matters and crimes committed in the colony. Travel and communication being what they were, officials at Louisbourg sometimes had to wait weeks or months for decisions on certain matters to arrive from France.

Île Royale and Louisbourg: Civil Population

Here is a roll-up summary of the census figures for the first twenty or so years of the colony's existence. The numbers show how quickly the population of Louisbourg grew after its founding. They also demonstrate the degree to which Louisbourg was the major population centre of Île Royale.

	1716	1720	1726	1734	1737	
Île Royale	1,472	2,630	3,131	3,407	3,938	
Louisbourg	510	633	951	1,116	1,463	
Louisbourg as % of Île Royale	35%	24%	30%	33%	37%	

Source: A. J. B. Johnston, *Control and Order at French Colonial Louisbourg* (37)

The setting is persuasive, so when the animators are convincing it's almost as if you are visiting Louisbourg back in 1744.

The other (roughly) two-thirds of Île Royale's civilian population lived in about a dozen smaller communities on the island, most of which were located along its eastern shore. Their resident populations tended to fluctuate sharply from census to census. Some of those outport villages were home to only a few dozen year-round residents, others to several hundred. The largest population outside of Louisbourg was at Niganiche (today's Ingonish). Census takers in 1737 recorded over seven hundred civilian residents in the northern Cape Breton port.

While migration to Louisbourg and the smaller communities on the island was large, natural increase certainly played a role. In 1720, children represented 22.4 per cent of Louisbourg's civilian population. In 1737, children represented 45.4 per cent of the total for civilians (664 of 1,463).

Chocolate

Chocolate was new to France in the late seventeenth century. Its first appearance in New France is at Quebec shortly before the founding of Louisbourg. Chocolate is found only five times in Louisbourg inventories, but it was very present in trade and other records. Its first documented use at Louisbourg was when it was given to soldiers who were diving to salvage a wrecked king's ship. The chocolate was meant to fortify them against the cold water. Many Europeans at the time regarded chocolate as a powerful "drogue." It could re-energize the elderly and the ill, but was too much for children and pregnant women. The popularity of chocolate grew quickly at Louisbourg, both as a trade item and as a beverage. One reason for this was the many Basque merchants at Louisbourg whose former home near the Spanish border was linked to an early chocolate production and distribution route.

Chocolate was first served as a hot drink, usually for breakfast, in a pot like the one above. It was combined with sugar and spices, melted in either hot water or hot milk, and frothed with a mill—a type of agitator—to make it creamier. With time, it was used to flavour pastry creams, and then found its way into desserts and pies, and even ice cream. At today's Fortress of Louisbourg, visitors can taste a recreation of eighteenth-century chocolate. The "reproduction," so to speak, was developed in cooperation with the Colonial Chocolate Society and Mars, Inc. It has the same flavour, melting point, and texture as early chocolate. It is made with whole cocoa beans, ground as it was in the eighteenth century, and combined with sugar and a few spices. Those interested in early chocolate recipes can find them in a new culinary history of Louisbourg, *French Taste in Atlantic Canada 1604–1758*, authored by Anne Marie Lane Jonah and Chantal Véchambre. *–Anne Marie Lane Jonah*

The cod fishery was the foundation upon which the Louisbourg economy was built.

The majority of the population on Île Royale was always French. Whether born in the colony or originally from Normandy, Brittany, the west coast, or elsewhere in France, a significant percentage of that population was Basque. They came from what was called the Basque country (*le pays basque*) in southwest France, adjacent to Spain. They spoke their own distinctive language (Basque), and had customs that sometimes set them apart.

The Basque language was not the only non-French language heard on the streets and wharves of Louisbourg. There were also those who spoke Breton (the ancient Celtic language of Brittany), and residents and visiting merchants who spoke English or Spanish. Then there were those French speakers from Acadia or Canada, or the French West Indies, whose accents and vocabularies might have surprised officials accustomed to

The Basques and Food

The southwestern French ports of Bayonne and St.-Jean-de-Luz near the Spanish border, and even a small town along the coast called Cap-Breton, were home to many of the seasonal fisheries workers in Louisbourg and elsewhere on Île Royale. Between 10 and 20 per cent of the permanent residents of Louisbourg were originally from that area.

Basques were among the leading merchants, as well as innkeepers, carpenters, and fishermen of Île Royale. Although many spoke French, they had a distinct language of their own, and tastes and clothing styles that set them apart. We can discern a few of their tastes and preferences from the written record of what they owned and traded. For instance, they liked strong, red Spanish wine from Navarre, chocolate, and *Jambon de Bayonne*, a dry-cured ham.

Basques have long had a special connection with chocolate, stemming from their connection with Spain. Jews fleeing Spanish religious repression regrouped in Bayonne and brought with them their trade of making chocolate, a new product the conquistadors had brought home from the Americas. It has been a defining industry of Bayonne, and it was a defining taste of the Basques in Louisbourg. On the other side of the ocean, of course, salt cod has always held a privileged place in Basque cuisine. *–Anne Marie Lane Jonah*

the French of a Paris salon. Additionally, there were Swiss and German soldiers of the Karrer Regiment in the Louisbourg garrison for over twenty years; and occasionally there were Mi'kmaw scouts in town, with their own language as well. Because it was a busy seaport, open to much of the Atlantic world, Louisbourg was, for its era, an extremely cosmopolitan place.

Louisbourg's emergence as an important military stronghold for France did not happen overnight. The stone fortifications erected at Louisbourg took over twenty years to build. At first, the idea was that there would be a simple line of defences along the landward front. Then, there were to be gun positions along the north shore (the Royal Battery) and on the island that guard-

Louisbourg harbour welcomed ships and boats of all sizes. Small shallops (*chaloupes*), such as this one, were principally used in the inshore fishery.

ed the harbour's narrow entrance (the Island Battery). Eventually, the engineers and the officials in France who approved the construction funds resolved to completely surround the town with walls and more than a hundred cannons and mortars. On the eve of Louisbourg's first war—which broke out in 1744—the heart of the town was completely surrounded by fortifications.

Of course, stone ramparts and artillery pieces are nothing without soldiers. Over time, as the town grew in size and

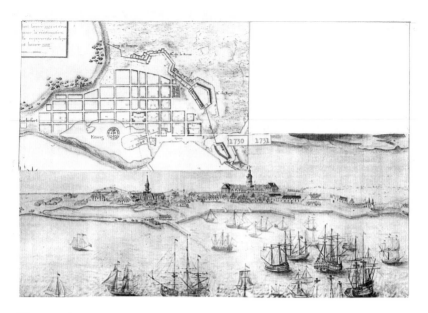

This combination of historical plans shows what the completely fortified town of Louisbourg looked like circa 1731.

importance and as the fortifications became steadily more complex, the size of the garrison at Louisbourg grew significantly. The largest single contingent was the Compagnies Franches de la Marine ("Independent Companies of the Ministry of the Marine"). By the 1740s there were eight companies of marine troops, with seventy men in each when they were at full strength. Next in size were the mercenaries of the Karrer Regiment, men from Switzerland and some of the German states. Many were Protestant, which made them oddities seeing as they were defending the Roman Catholic colony of a Roman Catholic monarch from a possible British Protestant attack. By the 1740s, there were about 150 Karrer soldiers at Louisbourg. The final members of the garrison at that time were thirty Canoniers-Bombardiers. They were the artillery specialists selected from the garrison as being capable of looking after the stronghold's 150 or so cannons and mortars.

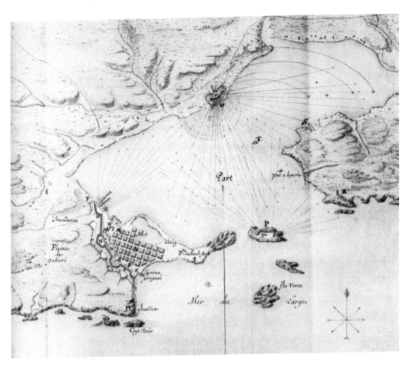

This plan, executed in the 1730s before Louisbourg was completely enclosed by fortifications on the ocean and harbour sides, shows the overlapping fields of artillery fire from the various positions around the defended harbour.

The impacts of the military presence on life at Louisbourg were many. Soldiers marched through the streets, had guardhouses throughout the town, stood guard in front of key buildings, and provided the equivalent of a nighttime police force. Once off-duty, they could be found pretty much everywhere, especially in cabarets. In fact, some of the disruptive elements and outright crime in Louisbourg were caused by off-duty soldiers. Excessive alcohol consumption—and related fights and thefts—was a constant problem.

On the left is a drummer for the Canoniers-Bombardiers. He is wearing the distinctive all-red cuffs, inner coat, breeches, and socks of his unit. On the right is a drummer for the Karrer Regiment. What is red on his fellow drummer is all yellow on his uniform. Both paintings are by renowned historical artist Francis Back.

Île Royale and Louisbourg: Civil and Military Populations Combined

When one combines the number of soldiers in the garrison with the civilian population, one gets an even clearer idea of the extent to which Louisbourg was by far the most populous town on Île Royale.

	1720	1726	1734	1737
Île Royale	2,947	3,581	3,957	4,524
Louisbourg	950	1,351	1,616	2,006
Louisbourg as % of Île Royale	32%	38%	41%	44%

Source: A. J. B. Johnston, *Control and Order at French Colonial Louisbourg* (38)

Entitled *Outbound from Louisbourg, 1744*, this painting by Peter Rindlisbacher depicts a ship under full sail heading out of the harbour. It captures the maritime dimension of the port. The ship in the foreground is based on *La Renommée*.

These numbers look small compared to the populations of North American cities today; however, in 1740, Quebec City had a population of about 4,600, Montreal around 4,200, and there were only between 60,000 and 70,000 people living in all of New York state. So Louisbourg was a sizeable settlement for the era. It was also one of the busiest seaports on the continent: an average of 150 vessels sailed in and out of the Louisbourg harbour each year.

This map situates Louisbourg within its geographical context of the Atlantic region and the Gulf of St. Lawrence.

Population of Louisbourg: Selected Years

Another way of breaking down Louisbourg's population is by gender and roles over time. Here is what the census data looks like from four different years.

	1720	1724	1734	1737
Habitants (heads of household)	69	113	159	163
Fishers	372	377	296	250
Servants (men & women)			137	229
Habitantes/Wives	50	84	128	157
Children	142	239	396	664
Total – Civil	633	813	1,116	1,463
Total – Military	317	430	552	543
Total – Civil and Military	950	1,243	1,668	2,006

Source: A. J. B. Johnston, *Control and Order at French Colonial Louisbourg* (39)

The fleur-de-lys was the symbol of the presence and power of the monarch. It appeared on any structure the royal purse had paid for.

Let us close this chapter by saying something about religion. One could make the case that religious attachments and rivalries were among the strongest forces in many European societies in the eighteenth century and earlier. Hundreds of thousands, if not millions, of lives were lost in wars and crusades conducted in the name of faith. On the other side of the equation, the responsibilities of churches in the bygone era typically went far beyond religious beliefs and morals; churches were also often the providers of health care, education, and many social services.

Louisbourg ended up with three separate religious groups. Two were male orders from France, and the third was a female religious community that came from Montreal. Each looked after a different aspect of religious and community life.

The Récollets of Brittany served as the parish priests and military chaplains at Louisbourg and elsewhere on Île Royale. They were the ones who kept all the parish records (baptisms, marriages, and burials) that were so important at the time and

Chapelle Saint-Louis in the King's Bastion Barracks served as the parish church of Louisbourg for most of the town's history. Because it was much too small to hold everyone for Mass, services had to be held at different times for the civilian and military population.

which, in recent years, have become so useful to historians and genealogists. The Récollets were on the payroll of the king, just like the royal officials and the military establishment. This meant that the cost of their salaries was not borne by the parishioners, which was much appreciated by the people of Louisbourg. Their frugality on such matters was exceptional for the era. Louisbourg may have been the only Roman Catholic community of its size in the world that rejected the idea of paying any kind of obligatory tithe to the church. In France the tithe was usually 1/13 of a person's income, in Canada (Quebec) it was 1/26. Yet at Louisbourg, the parishioners rejected any compulsory tithe at all.

There were two other ways in which religious practice at Louisbourg was unusual. There was no representative of the clergy on the local Superior Council (there was in Quebec), and the townspeople refused to contribute toward the construction of a bona fide church. Instead, they attended services in any of the

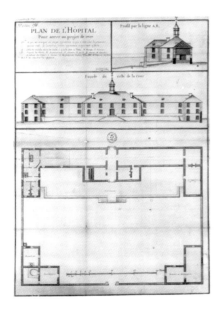

The hospital and its gardens and grounds occupied an entire block at Louisbourg. Its construction and operating costs were entirely paid by the king. Most of its patients were soldiers.

In the seventeenth century, Marguerite Bourgeoys founded the Congregation of Notre-Dame in Montreal as a teaching community for the education of girls. The first Sister from the congregation came to Louisbourg in 1727.

several chapels in town, which were paid for and maintained by the king. Thus, Louisbourg may well have been the most secular place in all of New France.

The second religious order at Louisbourg was the Brothers of Charity of the Order of St. John of God. Their specialty in France, Spain, and Italy had been in operating hospitals, which was what the Ministry of the Marine asked them to do on Île Royale. For over a decade, they operated an interim hospital on the north shore of Louisbourg harbour in the midst of the many fishing properties. Finally, in 1730, the Brothers moved into a massive hospital that had taken nine years to construct. Known as the King's Hospital—a clear indication of who paid for its

In this detail from his painting *View from the Clock Tower*, renowned historical artist Lewis Parker depicts one of the Brothers of Charity walking past a private dwelling, known in the reconstruction as the DeGannes House.

construction and its operating expenses—it was in the centre of the fortified town, and had four wards with twenty-five beds each, as well as a chapel, apothecary, bakery, kitchen, laundry, morgue, and other facilities.

The third religious group to come to Louisbourg was the Sisters of the Congregation of Notre-Dame. They dedicated themselves to providing education to girls. Unlike the two male orders, they were not brought to Île Royale by royal officials. They came as the result of a bold initiative by the bishop of Quebec and one of the Sisters; after she arrived in 1727 other Sisters came in the years that followed. The thinking was that the growing town needed someone to teach girls basic literacy skills and influence their morals.

Unfortunately for the Sisters, they would never receive the financial support provided to the Récollets and the Brothers of Charity. Consequently, the Congregation of Notre-Dame endured great hardships throughout their years in the colony.

The Widows of Louisbourg

Along the Louisbourg quay in 1744, four widows (*veuves*) operated their own businesses. Veuve Grandchamps ran an inn, Veuve Beauséjour ran Le Billard, a slightly better inn, Veuve Destouches a bakery, and Veuve Chevalier was a seamstress and ran a small boutique. There were also merchant widows in the town who ran fishing properties.

Why so many widows and why were they running businesses? Part of the answer is demographics. Because there were so many more men than women in the colony, women were, on average, considerably younger than men at the time of marriage. At Louisbourg, the average marriage ages were nineteen for women and twenty-nine for men; this increased the chance that wives would outlive their husbands. The other part of the answer was French law. The Custom of Paris (the law that governed civil life in Louisbourg), like other European codes at the time, considered women intellectually and morally "weak" and therefore needing to be governed by men. So fathers and husbands controlled women's lives and property. Widows, however, were an exception. They owned the inherited property and could act on their own behalf in business matters. In the eighteenth century, the home was often the place of business. Some wives took an active role, and were fully capable of taking over when their husbands died. Thus we find that in New France there were a significant number of *veuves* in business. –*Anne Marie Lane Jonah*

Nonetheless, virtually everyone praised what the Sisters were able to accomplish. An analysis of signatures on marriage documents found that women educated in the town were more literate than local men. There was no counterpart for boys at Louisbourg to what the Sisters offered to girls. A boy would only receive an education if his parents were able to hire a tutor.

We have established a basic overview of Louisbourg at its peacetime peak. It was a fortified French colonial seaport community with complexities and nuances that set it apart from the rest of New France. However, after thirty-one years of laying down a society that had experienced remarkable growth, that was about to change.

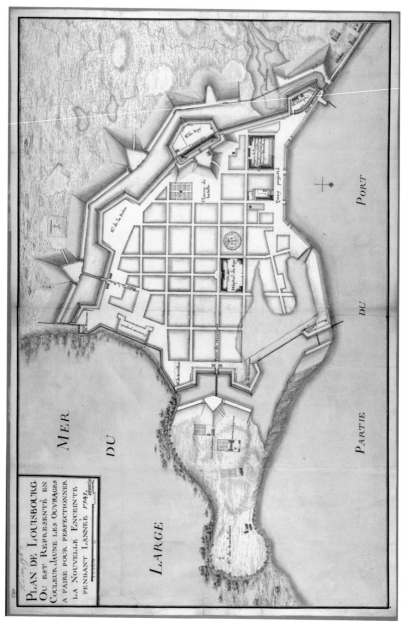

By the early 1740s, after nearly three decades of construction, Louisbourg was a fully enclosed fortified town.

CHAPTER 3

FIRST TIME AT WAR

It [Louisbourg] is shaped like an amphitheatre and commanded by various heights so that it can be raked with cannonballs and musketry so effectively that no one is safe there, neither in the houses nor in the streets.
–Jean-Pierre Roma, French colonist

FOR A century and a half, beginning in the early 1600s, the colonial era of what today are eastern Canada and the northeastern United States was marked by ongoing imperial rivalry between Great Britain and France. The Aboriginal peoples

This depiction of the Mi'kmaw warrior (left) is based on a historical description of one warrior's appearance. The Mi'kmaw woman is learning or reciting a prayer in a hieroglyphic prayer book held by a French missionary priest. Both illustrations are by Quebec historical artist Francis Back.

The Mi'kmaq as Allies of the French

There were specific reasons for the close ties between the Mi'kmaq and the French. By 1610, the Mi'kmaq had started to practice the Roman Catholic faith, thanks to activity by French missionaries stationed throughout Acadia. (Most English, on the other hand, were Protestant, in an era when religious differences were deeply felt.) There was also a limited amount of intermarriage between Acadians and Mi'kmaq, especially in the seventeenth century, which led to increasingly close ties for some.

Aboriginal warriors were feared and respected by all Europeans, and the French wanted them on their side. By the time Louisbourg was founded, the French were working hard to keep the Mi'kmaq and the Maliseet close to their cause. Louisbourg officials held special ceremonies each year to renew the alliance. An exchange of gifts and speeches formalized the link, and the French provided their Aboriginal allies with a range of needed supplies, including muskets and shot.

were involved as well. How could they not be? The territory being contested had once been exclusively theirs. The Mi'kmaq and the Maliseet—the two indigenous peoples in the Maritimes—were anything but pawns. They had interests all their own to pursue and to defend. It came down to questions of their survival, and the preservation of their resources, distinctive cultures, and ways of life. Before the final fall of Louisbourg in 1758, the Mi'kmaq regularly allied themselves with the French.

Overlapping and competing European and Aboriginal interests led to a series of wars in Atlantic Canada. For a long time, these conflicts were offshoots of campaigns that had begun in Europe and then spread overseas. By the 1750s, however, it was events in North America that were providing the first spark. Generally speaking, the size of the military forces of both the British and the French grew steadily larger as the years went by. So did what was at stake.

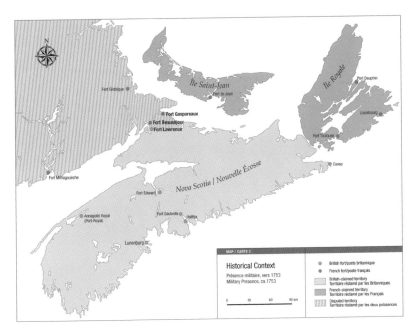

This map shows the areas of the Maritimes that were claimed by the British and the French in the early 1750s. It also names the major settlements. What the map does not show is the presence of the Mi'kmaq and the areas they controlled. This is because they moved around seasonally and did not establish towns and forts the way Europeans did.

From the Anglo-French perspective, the military rivalry came to a head in the middle of the eighteenth century. There were two wars with less than a decade between them: the War of the Austrian Succession (1740–48) and the Seven Years' War (1756–63). Not surprisingly, given the scale of the French investment at Louisbourg, the capital of Île Royale found itself in the heart of the conflict in both wars. In this chapter, our focus is on the first military action the town endured. (We'll turn to the second siege in Chapter 5.)

The soldiers of the Compagnies Franche de la Marine posted to Louisbourg had to practice marching and perform musketry drills on a regular basis.

During the thirty-one years of peace Louisbourg enjoyed after its founding in 1713, New England was both a major trading partner of the French colony and a potential military rival. The two regions were not far apart in the world of seagoing voyages, and Louisbourg's rival fishers were sometimes exploiting the same cod banks. Until war broke out in 1744, government officials and merchants at Louisbourg actively traded with the Anglo-American colonies for foodstuffs and construction materials. So-called "Boston boards" were widely used throughout the French town. So too, many New England vessels were sold at Louisbourg to French fishers and merchants.

Despite the active business relationship between Louisbourg and the British colonies in New England, there were many in New England who believed that, sooner or later, war would come between the mother countries—France and England—and when it did, Boston and Louisbourg would be on opposite sides. Some of those New Englanders felt that if they could hamper or even eliminate the French base, it would bring them prosperity. Many also saw Louisbourg as a potential military and naval threat. The fortified harbour on Cape Breton Island was—or rather could be, if war broke out—a base for French expeditions, warships, and privateers. Then, for some New Englanders, there was the matter of religion. To militant Protestants, the fact that the French colony was Roman Catholic was justification enough for something like a crusade. The era was one in which religious differences were often the cause of suspicion, condemnation, and outright war.

The tensions and rivalries that were long beneath the surface in the French Louisbourg-versus-British New England-relationship burst forth with deadly effect in 1744. In the spring of that year, Kings George II and Louis XV declared war on each other, the latest development in a European war that had been going on for several years. French privateers sailing out of Louisbourg began taking numerous Anglo-American

In 1744 a small contingent of French soldiers and a much larger force of Aboriginal allies made two attempts to besiege Annapolis Royal. This painting depicts an anxious nighttime moment in the first siege, as seen from the British perspective—that is, from inside the fort. Painting by Herb MacDonald.

prizes. French soldiers also led expeditions against what were then the only two English settlements in Nova Scotia. Canso, a New England fishing base on mainland Nova Scotia, fell easily to a Louisbourg-led expedition. Regrettably for the French, Annapolis Royal did not fall at all, despite the fact that many Mi'kmaq and Maliseet campaigned on the French side.

The French campaigns of 1744 greatly aggravated New Englanders. They viewed Nova Scotia as an extension or "outpost" of their colonies. There were cries for action against the French. A resident of Louisbourg would later write: "they [the New Englanders] might never have troubled us had we not affronted them first." During the winter of 1744–45, Governor William Shirley of Massachusetts proposed a strike against Louisbourg, arguing that nothing "would more effectually promote the interests of [Massachusetts]…than a reduction of that place." The vote was close—a one-vote victory after pressure from Boston merchants—but the Massachusetts legislature agreed to the proposal. Other Anglo-American colonies beyond Massachusetts soon joined in. New York, New Jersey, and Pennsylvania gave money, arms, and supplies. Sir William Pepperrell was selected to command the force. It was a striking example of intercolonial military cooperation. Some historians argue that the 1745 expedition that set off from the Thirteen Colonies to capture Louisbourg laid the groundwork for the Anglo-American colonists taking up arms as revolutionaries against Great Britain a generation later.

The Anglo-Americans knew that Louisbourg would not fall easily to them. Though most had not seen the place with their own eyes, they'd heard about it from those New England mariners who had. The mariners talked of many cannons and high, encircling stone walls. The actual figures were that Louisbourg had nearly three kilometres of perimeter walls, seven bastions, five guardhouses, four monumental gates, two outlying batteries, and more than one hundred cannons. By comparison, the more standard fortification in New England at that time was a simple blockhouse, a palisade, or an earthwork with a small battery of guns.

Benjamin Franklin wrote to his brother, who was about to besiege Louisbourg in 1745, that the Cape Breton fortress was going to be a "tough nut to crack and your teeth have not been accustomed to it." The British view—and the British supplied the 1745 expedition with vital naval support—was much the same.

Each unit and rank of the garrison wore distinctive colours and other unique touches. The braided cuff in this picture signifies that this uniform belonged to a drummer, as did the one behind it

A military officer named Philip Durell declared Louisbourg "certainly the strongest fortified Harbour I ever saw." Another British officer added that it was "much stronger than any place in England." He was wrong about that, but the comment nonetheless reveals some of the mystique surrounding Louisbourg at the time.

An encouraging rumour among the New England expedition as it readied to set off was that morale had been low among the troops at Louisbourg over the winter. Little did they know that the situation was worse for the French than they had heard: there had been a full-scale mutiny among the French troops only six months before.

The Mutiny at Louisbourg

In late December 1744, over the span of a couple hours on a Sunday morning, virtually every enlisted man in the Louisbourg garrison rose up in arms and took to the streets. Quickly and completely, they assumed control of the entire town. Various grievances lay behind the uprising. There were complaints about uniforms, firewood, poor food, and rations not being received. There was also the matter that the commandant of the May 1744 attack on Canso had told the soldiers who volunteered that they would receive a share of the booty. They had not received a thing.

These various issues came to a head in the early morning hours of December 27, when the Swiss and German soldiers of the mercenary Karrer Regiment assembled in the courtyard of the King's Bastion, and demanded their complaints be addressed. Not long after, the French soldiers of the marine companies joined the protest, giving it a much more militant thrust. The authorities had no choice but to give in to the soldiers' demands; there were no other French troops who could be brought to bear against the mutineers. Moreover, the mutinous soldiers let it be known that they could pillage the town and hand the colony over to the enemy the following spring, if they so chose.

Though they yielded to the soldiers' demands, the authorities at Louisbourg would neither forgive nor forget. The leaders of the mutiny would pay with their lives when the coming siege of 1745 was over.

In round figures, four thousand New Englanders set sail in the spring of 1745 to attack Louisbourg. The campaigners were all "amateur" soldiers in the sense that they were volunteers and not part of a professionally trained year-round force. Nonetheless, some of the officers and enlisted men had been involved in previous wars or campaigns. As to why they were taking part in the expedition, facing possible injury or death, the motivations ranged from a hope for booty, to a sense of economic rivalry with a French colony, to territorial ambition, to religious fervour.

This painting of action at sea off Louisbourg during the 1745 siege empha-
sizes the role and contribution of the British, not the New Englanders. The
Royal Navy provided crucial naval support and enforced a blockade. The
army that carried out the besieging was from New England.

Although Gov. William Shirley was the driving force behind the expedition, he did not go along. William Pepperrell
from Kittery, Maine, commanded the land force. An experienced British naval officer, Commodore Peter Warren, was in
charge of the fleet, which consisted of twelve British warships
and about one hundred New England vessels. Some were troop
transports and others carried the necessary provisions to support

Two Calendars in Play

Until 1752, Great Britain and its colonies followed the Julian calendar, which was eleven days behind the more astronomically correct Gregorian calendar followed in France and most other European countries. This means that when the New Englanders took possession of Louisbourg on what was, according to their calendar, June 17, 1745, the French considered it June 28. When Britain finally made the calendar switch in 1752, some people rioted because they thought they were being cheated of eleven days of their lives.

the campaign. No one knew if the venture would succeed, and if so, how long it would take. Their rendezvous point prior to blockading and then besieging Louisbourg was Canso, Nova Scotia, which the French had captured and then burned the previous year.

When the acting governor of Île Royale, Louis Du Pont Duchambon, learned that an attacking force was headed his way, he assembled the soldiers of the garrison. He appealed to them to drop their mutinous spirit and unite with their officers and the civilian population to defend the town against the approaching enemy. The soldiers wanted a guarantee that there would be no punishment for having taken part in the mutiny, and they received the assurances they sought. Yet we wonder from our vantage point two and a half centuries later, did the officers fully trust the men in their command? Or did they rule out certain options, like sorties beyond the walls, because they lacked confidence in their men?

The French garrison numbered fewer than seven hundred soldiers with an additional possibility of nine hundred civilians in an untrained militia. This meant the French defenders were less than half as many as the New England force.

The besiegers from New England came ashore along Gabarus Bay on May 11, 1745 (according to the Gregorian calendar).

In this painting by an unknown French officer—almost certainly an engineer—we see the Royal Battery in the foreground, and the threatening fleet of British and New England ships beyond the harbour entrance.

The French sent out a force to oppose them, but it was too little, too late. Because the enemy was now ashore, the French abandoned one of their defences, the Royal Battery, since the New England soldiers could easily attack it from the rear. The fleeing soldiers spiked the guns, thinking they would be useless to the New Englanders. However, the spiking was poorly done, and before too long the enemy had repaired the cannons and began to use them to bombard the fortress.

The siege was to last for nearly seven weeks. At the same time, a squadron of British warships blockaded the entrance to Louisbourg harbour, ensuring no French ships could enter the port to bring relief in the form of supplies or reinforcements. The bloodiest battle during the siege occurred on June 6, 1745, when the New Englanders made a direct assault on the Island Battery. The French defenders unleashed a deadly fire that cost many New England lives. The Island Battery did not fall in that battle. Soon after, however, the besiegers began to bombard that same island position from a battery set up on Lighthouse Point. Eventually, this did the trick, and the French had to withdraw back into the fortress.

What Happened to the People of Louisbourg?

The French administration, colonists, and soldiers were transported to France—specifically to ports on the west coast. They would spend the next four years awaiting the outcome of the war, to see if perhaps they might be returning to Île Royale if it were handed back in a peace treaty.

Despite the assurances given on the eve of the 1745 siege, authorities in France undertook proceedings against the ringleaders of the December 1744 mutiny. Separate trials were held, for the soldiers of the Compagnies Franches de la Marine and the men of the Karrer Regiment. In the end, four Karrer soldiers and eight men of the marine troops were found guilty of inciting a mutiny. One escaped, eight were executed, two were given life sentences to the galleys of the Mediterranean, and one died in prison.

The French defenders held out as long as they could, but they were outgunned by the New England army and lacked sufficient naval ships of their own to disrupt the British blockade. The situation that military engineers had warned about thirty years before had come true. Louisbourg's defences were commanded by nearby heights of land—the amphitheatre effect of which Jean-Pierre Roma wrote—from which the enemy batteries rained down cannonballs and mortar bombs.

The end came in late June. The New England gun batteries moved ever closer to the walls of the town and were able to silence every cannon on the French side, while inflicting serious damage to the fortifications and many houses within. On June 27, the two sides negotiated surrender terms. The British and New England troops marched in the next day. Because of the bombardment of the western entrance to the town, the victors could not enter by the Dauphin Gate: it had been turned into a mass of rubble. Instead, the New Englanders came into Louisbourg by the Queen's Gate on the southern front. According to an eyewitness, they entered "with Colours...flying, the Drums Beating,

Trumpets Sounding, Flutes & Viols Playing." The music was to celebrate what, for the besiegers, was a joyous event.

Inside Louisbourg, another eyewitness recorded: "most of the Houses, which are two hundred and fifty, are demolished, or very much shattered, which makes lodging very uncomfortable. Here was a fine Church, which is intirely [sic] destroyed by the Shot." Most of those buildings could and would be restored or rebuilt, but not by the French. It would be up to the soldiers taking over the town.

The British and New England victors at Louisbourg soon sent away every inhabitant they could round up, from Louisbourg and every other community on Île Royale, on ships to France. This amounted to a forcible removal; a deportation—though that word is not commonly used to describe it—of several thousand inhabitants. The New England expeditionary force, with the important assistance of a British naval squadron, had accomplished what they had set out to do: they had put an end to the French economic and territorial bastion on Cape Breton Island. As part of the victory, Île Saint-Jean (Prince Edward Island) also went to the winning side.

The ordinary soldiers from New England had not planned on remaining at Louisbourg beyond the campaign; they thought once the place was captured they would be going home. That is not how it worked out. Having captured Louisbourg, the leaders of the expedition had to garrison the fortified town in case the French tried to take it back. This risk would exist until a peace treaty was signed signalling the end of the war and the fate of Louisbourg was decided one way or another. So that meant the New Englanders were going to have to stay on through the winter, at least until the spring of 1746.

That first winter at Louisbourg killed about nine times as many soldiers as the fighting had done over the nearly seven weeks of the siege. Roughly one hundred New Englanders died during the siege, and approximately nine hundred died in the

The Terrible Winter of 1745–46

A powerful storm swept the shores of the Fortress of Louisbourg in February 2006, exposing the long-buried remains of several eighteenth-century structures, including the corner of a small stone foundation on the north shore of Rochefort Point (the small peninsula that extends beyond the east gate of the fortress). Once the storm passed, archaeologists surveyed the shoreline, located the stone feature, and began a rescue excavation. The operation revealed a surprising truth hidden behind the rough stone walls: the feature turned out to be the root cellar of a house destroyed during the siege of 1745. Within the cellar lay forty-three skeletons atop the burnt beams and chimney rubble that spilled across the floor. The skeletons had been neatly laid. There were two layers of shroud burials arranged head to toe, covered with large slabs of limestone that had come from a nearby lime kiln. The arrangement was then capped with a thick layer of loose beach sand. Many hundreds of New Englanders perished at Louisbourg during that terrible winter of 1745–46, and this cellar-cum-mass grave was one of the locations where the Anglo-American garrison buried their dead. They did the best they could, in a desperate yet practical manner. No one at the time had written of this burial location and no folklore had remembered it. It took 260 years for the ocean to bring this story back to us. Fortunately, we were there to receive it.
—*Rebecca Dunham*

1731 Rochefort Point, Louisbourg

months that followed. The killers were diseases and a total lack of preparedness for what turned out to be an extremely harsh winter.

The New Englanders were eventually relieved of the responsibility of occupying Louisbourg by the British army. In 1746 France did send out a massive expedition, led by the Duc d'Anville, to re-establish its presence in the Atlantic region, but the campaign was devastated by storms and disease. The French armada was a disaster and had no effect on the British control of Louisbourg. British regulars would remain at what had been France's Atlantic stronghold until the summer of 1749.

The best way to convey how awful the British and New England occupation of Louisbourg was is to offer the following description. It was penned by the new British governor of Cape Breton Island, Charles Knowles, after he suffered through the terrible winter of 1746.

Words are wanting to represent the severity of the weather. Causes great suffering and misery among the troops. Many have froze [sic] to death, and the sentries, though relieved every half hour frequently lose their toes and fingers, some have lost their limbs by mortification in a few hours. The houses and quarters in general are bad and do not help keep out snow and cold. Both officers and men have little comfort even within doors. No sense in exercising to keep warm, as the snow can reach levels of 10, 12, 16 feet in depth. When it stops snowing, the island is covered in a sheet of ice. Nothing is more common than for one guard to dig the other out of the guardroom before they can relieve them. The drift snow sometimes covers houses entirely. On fortifications: very poor condition. The summer, where most repairs were to be done, saw only 5 fair days together without some alteration. For every 5, we had 12–14 days of drizzle, rain, and fog. The men die faster than they can be recruited (to form new regiments). We cannot bury our dead but are forced to let them lay in the snow till the thaws come.

In another epistle, Knowles described Louisbourg as the "worst spot on the Globe."

The next twist in the tale of Louisbourg—a peacetime resurgence in French hands again—was to occur first in late 1748, and then, in full, in the summer of 1749.

The cone-shaped building is an icehouse. Within it was a well where ice was placed in winter. Because the place was always cool, it was where the governor and other notables kept perishable foods.

CHAPTER 4

RETURN AND FLOURISH

Though war had taken Louisbourg, Île Royale, and Île Saint-Jean from France, the regime of Louis XV maintained every hope of getting the two islands back through the peace that would bring an end to the conflict. Ultimately, this is how all wars end, with treaties negotiated by the two or more sides involved. The war in question took place not only in North America. The French and the British also fought and had interests in Europe, India, and Africa. War, by this period, had become a vast imperial game. When it came to making peace, assets in one area might be traded away for assets somewhere else.

The French had not the slightest doubt that they had suffered an enormous loss when Louisbourg fell to the enemy in 1745. The busy port and the larger colony of Île Royale had been important cogs in the French colonial trading network, which in turn had contributed greatly to the overall economy of France. The Île Royale fishery formed only a part of the overall North Atlantic fishery, but it was extremely significant by itself. Cod exports from Île Royale averaged between two and three million livres a year—approximately twice the value of fur exports from Canada during the same period.

This illustration comes from an eighteenth-century book on the cod fishery. In a single frame, it illustrates the cod being brought to an onshore structure where the fish was split and processed. It would then be taken out to dry on beach stones and "flakes"—the wooden platforms shown out in the open air. Once dried, the fish were stacked on the circular shapes in the background before being shipped away.

In the specific case of Louisbourg, the fortified harbour was not only a place for fishing boats and bountiful catches of cod. During times of peace, there was a large and lucrative merchant trade. As noted earlier, ships from France, the French West Indies, Canada, and New England regularly came and went. These many vessels either sold or exchanged commodities from their regions (like molasses, rum, sugar, and tobacco from the West Indies) to obtain dried cod, or commodities from Europe and beyond. Louisbourg had established itself as a centre of trade and transshipment. Not surprisingly, the French negotiators of the peace treaty that was to end the War of the Austrian Succession wanted to get that port back into their hands. They were eager to re-establish the economic network that had existed before the war, and if that meant trading away valuable assets somewhere else, that was a price they were willing to pay.

The drawn-out negotiations took place at the German city of Aachen (then known to the French as Aix-la-Chapelle). The Treaty of Aix-la-Chapelle was finally signed in late 1748. Possessions captured during the war were to be returned to their previous masters. (The term used to describe such a reversion is *status quo ante bellum*.) In other words, Great Britain agreed to return Louisbourg and Île Royale back to France, while France agreed to withdraw its troops from several strategic border towns in the Low Countries that it had captured during the war. Many authors have gone into print saying Louisbourg was exchanged for Madras, India, but that is not what a close analysis of the treaty suggests. The relationship was between Louisbourg and the border towns in what is now Belgium. Madras was indeed handed over to the British by the French at the same time, but the exchange was not for Louisbourg.

The peace treaty delighted the French, especially those living in coastal regions where fishery and trade were important. Some people in Britain, on the other hand, said that it was a great mistake for their diplomats to give away Louisbourg. In a not-too-distant future, they argued, the British army and Royal Navy would have to capture the Cape Breton stronghold again. But the strongest negative reaction was in New England. Many in that region were furious to see the mother country give away their great conquest of 1745. It had been a source of immense pride. (To this day, there's an urban park in Boston's Beacon Hill named Louisburg Square, after the victory.) Nearly a thousand of New England's provincial soldiers had perished at Louisbourg in the winter that followed the siege. The British decision to hand

An Astronomical Observatory at Louisbourg

Aside from having Canada's first lighthouse, Louisbourg was also home to the country's first observatory. French scientist Joseph-Bernard Chabert de Cogolin was in the colony in 1750–51 to take astronomical readings, so as to improve the accuracy of French maps and charts. Although latitude was well understood, no one had yet solved the puzzle of longitude, and Chabert de Cogolin contributed to that field of study. His main observation point was a small wooden building erected on the ramparts of the King's Bastion, within which he and his assistant trained their telescopes on the sky.

over the French stronghold greatly annoyed and alienated many in New England. Historians have argued that Great Britain's return of Louisbourg to France in 1748 helped sow the seeds of anti-British sentiment that would swell during the 1760s and 1770s and eventually lead to the American Revolution.

Louisbourg and Île Royale were handed back too late in 1748 for the colonial authorities in France to send out ships and colonists to re-occupy the place. Winter crossings of the Atlantic Ocean were risky undertakings, and not to be attempted unless the situation was desperate. Thus, the re-establishment of the

This map of Halifax in the 1750s was drawn, secretly, by a French officer who was a prisoner in the town. The officer was at liberty to stroll around during the day, which he did, and he compiled a map of what he saw. He tried to covertly send the detailed map to Louisbourg, but it was found folded up inside a ball of soap.

French at Louisbourg and in the smaller communities of Île Royale had to wait until the fairer sailing weather of 1749.

As it turned out, the French return to Louisbourg would be only one of two pivotal events in the history of Atlantic Canada during the summer of 1749. The other was the founding of Halifax. The two events occurred within a few days of each other, which was no coincidence. The British established Halifax as a military base on mainland Nova Scotia precisely

Kjipuktuk Becomes Halifax

In selecting a harbour for their new stronghold, the British chose the large anchorage known to the Mi'kmaq for centuries as Kjipuktuk. Early in the eighteenth century, before the 1713 Treaty of Utrecht, a French engineer had urged his nation to settle at the harbour, which he called Chibouquetou. The engineer even sketched what fortifications were required.

In 1746 the harbour was the place of rendezvous for the Duc d'Anville and his ill-fated French armada. When the British arrived in 1749, they renamed the place Halifax to honour George Montague Dunk, earl of Halifax. As president of the Board of Trade in England, Dunk had played the leading role in supporting the project. Had they selected the man's family name, Halifax might have been called Dunktown instead.

because the French were again in possession of Cape Breton Island and Louisbourg. They felt they needed a counterbalance to the stronghold and threat they saw in the capital of Île Royale. Prior to the establishment of Halifax, there were only two tiny English settlements—Annapolis Royal and Canso—in all of Nova Scotia. The rest of the territory was either controlled by the Mi'kmaq or settled by the Acadians. Without a formidable stronghold, the British reasoned, all of Nova Scotia might eventually be lost to the French.

While the British worried about losing the region to the French, the French feared the success of what the British planned to achieve at their new base at Halifax. A senior official at Quebec, François Bigot (formerly the financial administrator at Louisbourg), wrote succinctly of the founding of Halifax: "If that establishment proves successful, we can abandon [any hope of regaining] Acadia."

The British expedition to establish a base at Halifax consisted of a flotilla of thirteen transports, accompanied by a sloop-of-war. Together they carried 2,576 settlers, a large majority of

In this image, the fledgling settlement of Halifax is being literally carved out of the forest by its settlers in 1749. In the beginning, Halifax was completely surrounded by a palisade and five log forts, due to a fear of attacks by the Mi'kmaq and/or the French.

whom were adult males. Right away, houses and other shelters were erected. At the same time, the settlement had to be ready to defend itself. Blockhouses were erected at strategic locations around the harbour, including five log forts, which were linked by a palisade of pickets surrounding the main settlement.

A few days before that British expedition reached what was soon to be called Halifax Harbour, the French arrived off the rocky coast near Louisbourg. Their flotilla consisted of two men-of-war, a convoy of transports bearing the civilian population and a contingent of soldiers, and a frigate drawing up the rear. A small delegation went ashore to begin the negotiations with the

This scene was painted by Hibbert Newton Binney in the late eighteenth century, and reflects the kind of clothing the Mi'kmaq were wearing at that time.

British administration. It took a few weeks of discussion to work out all the details for transferring the colony of Île Royale from one imperial power to the other. The incoming French civilian population numbered just under two thousand men, women, and children.

Most of the French civilians making the crossing to Louisbourg in 1749 were either returning to their place of birth, or to the place where they had lived before being removed in 1745. The town had suffered during the siege, but the New Englanders and the British had made some repairs and alterations. There were also a few new major buildings, notably a brewery and a barracks. Though the changes were important

The View of the Mi'kmaq

It is important to recall that the territory within which both the French and the British were making plans and building forts and towns had, since time immemorial, belonged to the Mi'kmaq. While the Mi'kmaq generally had harmonious relations with the Acadians and the French, that was not the case with the British. When the Mi'kmaq chiefs learned about what was happening at Kjipuktuk (Halifax), they composed an eloquent letter of protest written in Mi'kmaq and French. Here is a portion of that letter, translated into English:

The place where you are, where you are building dwellings, where you are now building a fort, where you want, as it were, to enthrone yourself, this land of which you wish to make yourself now absolute master, this land belongs to me. I have come from it as certainly as the grass, it is the very place of my birth and of my dwelling, this land belongs to me, the Native person, yes I swear, it is God who has given it to be my country for ever…you drive me out; where do you want me to take refuge? You have taken almost all this land in all its extent.

to individual owners whose properties were affected, the layout of the fortifications was essentially the same as it had been four years before. Not surprisingly, the British weren't handing over a place they had made stronger. Having lost the place once, the French recognized that Louisbourg would have to be made more formidable—and house more soldiers—in case there was another siege. Of that probability, few had any doubt. Practically everyone on both sides viewed the Treaty of Aix-la-Chapelle not as a lasting peace, but as a temporary truce.

Unlike in 1713, when Louisbourg was founded without much pomp, the 1749 re-founding was celebrated with great pageantry, and over a period of several days. There were drum rolls, booming artillery salutes, and assembled lines of troops. The union flag of Great Britain was lowered and the white flag

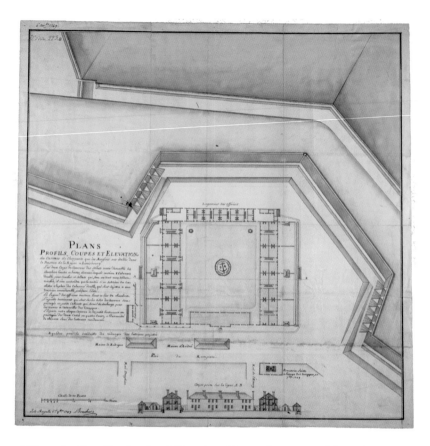

When the New England and British soldiers who occupied Louisbourg in the late 1740s sailed away in July 1749, they left behind a barracks they had constructed. The French took over the rectangular, two-storey barracks, and used it during the 1750s.

of France raised in its place. A *Te Deum*, the ancient Latin hymn of thanksgiving, was sung in the military chapel that served as the town's parish church, with one thousand soldiers on the nearby ramparts and *place d'armes*. At the conclusion of the *Te Deum*, the soldiers fired three rounds from their muskets and offered a twenty-one-gun salute.

Yet another massive ceremony was held when the French vessels returned from helping transport the British troops to Halifax. They brought with them the remains of the Duc d'Anville, who had perished at Halifax in 1746 and been interred on Georges Island. His remains were carried back to Louisbourg and, with accompanying artillery salutes, placed beneath the floor of the Chapelle Saint-Louis, where two previous governors of Île Royale had also been buried.

The life of the parish at Louisbourg—Notre-Dame-des-Anges—began again as soon as the French came ashore. Because the population started off at around two thousand and grew from there, the parish priests—the Récollets—were busier than their predecessors had been. Over the span of the next ten years, the parish would host 1,114 baptisms, 332 marriages, and 579 burials. These numbers almost speak for themselves. They reveal the size and scale of a community that was a full-fledged town and not simply a large fortification.

Just as the Récollets returned as the parish priests and chaplains, so too did the Brothers of the Charity to run the King's Hospital, and the Sisters of the Congregation of Notre-Dame to once again to open a school for girls. Sadly, as before, the Sisters were beset by financial difficulties. These problems were made worse when a hurricane blew down a new school they were building.

On the military front, the authorities in France sent one thousand Compagnies Franches soldiers to Louisbourg in 1749. The artillery specialists, the Canoniers-Bombardiers, were sent back as well. The authorities would not, however, bring back any of the Karrer Regiment; they blamed those Swiss and German mercenaries for sparking the mutiny of 1744. Instead, beginning in 1755, France sent battalions of infantry regiments from the French army to Louisbourg. Two contingents—of the Artois and Bourgogne Regiments—arrived in 1755. Two more—of the Cambis and Volontaires Étrangers Regiments—reached

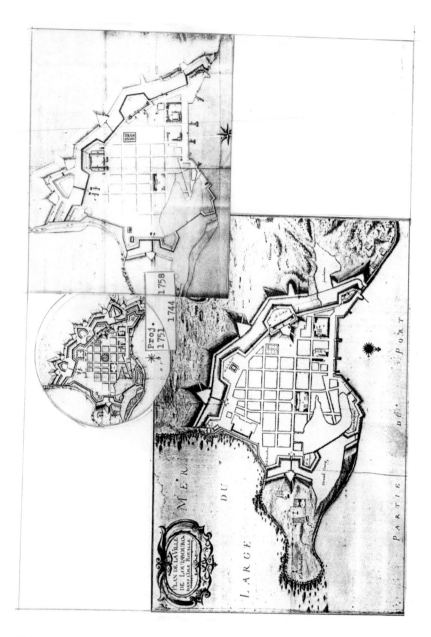

This combination of map images shows the full extent of the fortifications that surrounded the main portion of the town of Louisbourg. As a walled city, it represented a veritable stronghold for the Atlantic aspirations of France.

Louisbourg in 1758, just before the second siege began. This meant that Louisbourg had about 3,500 professionally trained soldiers in the garrison in time for the next siege. That was roughly five times as many defenders as had been there in 1745.

In addition to improving the manpower situation, the royal government in France also authorized repairs to the old fortifications, as well as a few new additions to improve defensibility. New batteries were situated on Lighthouse and Rochefort Points, and a large outer work was constructed along the shore near Black Rock. The price tag for all the work, plus all the extra soldiers, was significant. But then, the stakes were as high as they could be. Louisbourg and Île Royale were key cogs in France's imperial system, and the authorities were willing to pay a high price to keep them.

PLAN DE
LOUISBOURG.
Echelle.

Ouvrage exécuté pendant le Siege

150 Toises

RENVOIS
DU PLAN DE LOUISBOURG,
dans L'Isle Royale, au Canada.

1. Ouvrages projettés.
2. Porte de la Reine.
3. Place d'Armes.
4. Porte Dauphine.
5. Porte de Maurepas.
6. Pointe de Rochefort.
7. Cap Noir.
8. Lac, qui sert de Port en hiver.

Tentative inutile des Anglois sur Louisbourg, le 7. Sept.bre 1757.
Le 26. Juillet, en 1758. Louisbourg se rend, aux Anglois.

Though extensive repairs were carried out after the French returned to Louisbourg in 1749, the fortified town was not much stronger than it had been in 1745. An outer work was added on the southern side (near the compass rose) of town, as well as new batteries on Lighthouse and Rochefort Points. The latter is shown at number 6.

CHAPTER 5

AN END AND A BEGINNING

Our landing was next to miraculous.... I wouldn't recommend the Bay of Gabarouse for a descent, especially as we managed it. –James Wolfe, after the British came ashore at Louisbourg on June 8, 1758.

JUST IN case it was not obvious from the preceding chapter, let us make it clear: the shadow of another war with Great Britain dominated all aspects of life at Louisbourg after the 1749 arrival of the civilian population and the soldiers to defend them.

As we have seen, Versailles authorized great sums of money to be spent on the reparation and improvement of the fortifications, and on sending many more troops to Louisbourg than had ever been there before. The idea was that if and when there was a second siege, Louisbourg might be able to withstand it, and thereby continue to contribute to the economic and imperial aspirations of France.

Yet, as we shall see, when all was said and done, Louisbourg would fall a second time. One of the key actions leading to that defeat would occur off the coast of France, thousands of kilometres away from the Cape Breton stronghold, and months before the siege would even begin. But we're getting ahead of ourselves.

A fresh war between Great Britain and France was officially declared in 1756, though hostilities and acts of war were already taking place in parts of North America. Two of the most notable examples are the British capture of the French fort at Beauséjour in 1755, and the first of the forcible

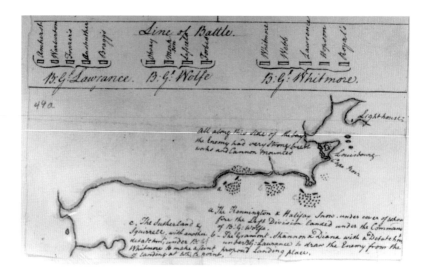

This British sketch, found in a manuscript, shows the June 8, 1758, landing at Anse de la Cormorandière. Three flotillas of small boats are shown heading for shore, down the coast from the heavily fortified peninsula of Louisbourg on the right.

removals of thousands of Acadians in the months that followed. While those actions were taking place on land, squadrons of British Royal Navy ships were actively intercepting French vessels that carried soldiers and provisions destined for Quebec and Louisbourg. The British were also carrying out months-long blockades of Louisbourg harbour. They could not prevent all maritime communication between mother country and colony, but they made enough seizures to severely affect French shipping costs, insurance rates, fisheries, commerce, and military preparedness. The financial administrator of Île Royale described the situation at Louisbourg in late 1756.

We can no longer rely absolutely on the commerce of France or that of Canada for the subsistence of the colony. It's from the storehouses of the King that people today generally draw flour and all that they need to live.... If there is not always enough [foodstuffs] for two years in advance in the storehouses of the King during the war, we will be obliged to withdraw the population and famine will follow.

Similar assessments would be penned in 1757 and early 1758.

After the Seven Years' War began in earnest, the British commitment to cut off Louisbourg from its sources of ships, soldiers, and supplies was intensified. Life in the town became more difficult as time went by. The authorities in France had to resort to sending reinforcements and provisions at times of year when there would be no British blockades off the coast. That meant ocean crossings in late autumn, mid-winter, and early spring, when bad weather and roiling seas were the main risks.

Though there was nothing anyone at Louisbourg could do about the Royal Navy's dominance on the high seas—only France's navy could try to influence that situation—the authorities in the town did resolve to prepare for an assault they expected to come sooner or later. They set out to strengthen the existing fortifications and, just as importantly, establish new ones at the landing places along the coast where the British might try to come ashore. The most important work was undertaken in the summer of 1757.

In 1757 three separate French squadrons eluded Royal Navy flotillas and reached Louisbourg. This was made possible not because the British had relaxed their blockade, but due to logistical problems that kept their ships out of the waters of Atlantic Canada early in the shipping season. The first French ships sailed into Louisbourg in late May, and the other two squadrons arrived in mid-June. All together, eighteen French ships of the line made it to Louisbourg that summer. It was an assembly of sails and sailors such as had never before been seen at Louisbourg and, unfortunately for the French, would not be seen again.

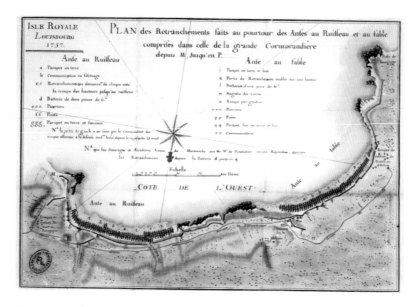

This detailed plan shows the full extent of French defensive preparations at Anse de la Cormorandière, where the British would come ashore a year later. The plan shows the tree and branch obstructions (*abatis*) on the beaches, and the soldiers and small artillery positions facing the shore. The British would rename the area Kennington Cove in 1758, after the ship that began the bombardment on June 8, 1758.

The individual in command of the overall French flotilla was a legendary figure in French naval circles. His name was Emmanuel-August de Cahideuc, comte du Bois de la Motte, a seventy-four-year old veteran of many battles and campaigns. Over the course of his stay in the capital of Île Royale that summer, Du Bois de la Motte transformed the way in which Louisbourg was defended. His emphasis, unlike that of his predecessors, was on preventing the enemy from getting ashore in the first place. This had not been the case in 1745, when an army from New England had easily landed on the shoreline near Louisbourg and then besieged the fortified town over the six weeks that followed. Before 1757, there had been modest attempts at introducing some coastal defences beyond the main fortifications of Louisbourg, but nothing of much significance had been accomplished. This seventy-four-year old naval commandant would change all that. First, however, Du Bois de la Motte had a medical crisis among his fleet to endure.

In the eighteenth century, it was common when ships reached port after a long voyage that some of the crew would need medical attention. The summer of 1757 at Louisbourg, however, presented a severe challenge. Unbeknownst to the naval commanders when their ships left France, a few sailors were carrying typhus. By the time the ships dropped anchor in Louisbourg harbour, there were so many sick sailors that they could not all be accommodated in the King's Hospital. Some of the sick were placed in twenty-four houses located outside the walls of the town. This was done to reduce the chances of the disease spreading within the town. But despite such precautions, the typhus situation became progressively worse. Eventually it resulted in a huge death toll, especially in coastal France in late 1757.

While typhus raged at Louisbourg, Du Bois de la Motte and the town's military leadership put all available men—soldiers, sailors off ships, and civilians—to work. They spent months erecting defences and manning positions in case the British—who were by then offshore in their usual blockade—tried to come ashore. At times there were three thousand men-at-arms—mostly regular soldiers, but also several hundred Aboriginal warriors, a force of irregulars, and a smaller number of Acadian partisans—camping and standing guard at the various potential landing beaches. The most heavily defended location was Anse de la Cormorandière (Kennington Cove). As fate would have it, that cove would be the very spot where the British would attempt to come ashore one year later, in June 1758.

The British fleet that was offshore from Louisbourg in that same summer of 1757 had every intention of besieging

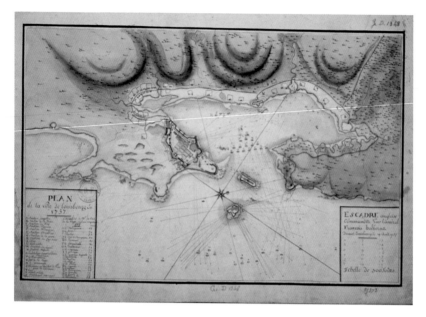

This plan depicts the situation in the late summer of 1757, when a squadron of French ships within Louisbourg harbour were the match of a squadron of British ships just outside the harbour mouth. In this instance, no British assault was attempted. But the next year, when the British flotilla greatly outnumbered the French ships at Louisbourg, there would be a landing, and a siege to follow.

and capturing the place. The 1757 expedition, led by Admiral Francis Holburne and Lord Loudoun, was roughly the same size as the expedition that would attack Louisbourg the following year—the one that wrote its way into so many history books with its success. So what happened in 1757 that kept the British from even attempting a landing on the beaches near Louisbourg? Holburne and Loudoun decided that the eighteen French warships in Louisbourg harbour matched their own flotilla, meaning that their troops would not be able to get ashore and overwhelm the town. As a result, the British did not even attempt a landing, but contented themselves with blockading the harbour as they had been doing for several years.

The impasse continued for weeks. Then, in September, a hurricane badly damaged both flotillas: the British along the Cape Breton coastline and the French within Louisbourg harbour. The windstorm effectively ended the unsuccessful 1757 British campaign against Louisbourg. In the weeks that followed, the three French squadrons returned to France with large numbers of their sailors sick with typhus. On arrival at the naval port of Brest and its nearby region, the death toll on the ships was in the thousands.

In the aftermath of their unsuccessful expedition to capture Louisbourg, the senior military leadership in Great Britain, including Prime Minister William Pitt, assessed what had gone wrong. They learned that the British force had taken too long to get across the Atlantic, and that when it did get there, the three sizeable French squadrons already in the harbour nullified the expedition's chance of success. To prevent a repeat, the British resolved to do things differently in 1758.

One innovation for 1758 was the idea to overwinter a number of warships in Halifax, so as to get an early start on blockading the French stronghold at Île Royale. Overwintering was an important step toward turning Halifax into a major overseas naval port for the British. That role grew immeasurably after the American Revolution brought about the loss of their Anglo-American ports. Halifax would, in fact, remain an important port and naval station for the British until 1906, when the Canadian government took over the port's installations.

A second innovation—the one referred to near the beginning of this chapter—was the decision by the British to blockade the three French naval ports, to prevent as many French warships as possible from reaching Louisbourg. That was what had thwarted the British expedition of 1757. Accordingly, beginning in early 1758, there were British naval squadrons off

Rochefort, France, a short distance up the Charente River, was one of three French naval bases in the eighteenth century. The others were Brest and Toulon. Among other features, Rochefort had dry docks for the construction and repair of warships, and a large factory for the fabrication of rope.

Brest and Rochefort on France's Atlantic coast, and near Toulon on the Mediterranean. In taking these actions thousands of kilometres from Louisbourg, the British lay the foundation for the victory that was to come.

The Royal Navy squadrons cruising in French waters dramatically altered the course of the war. The British could not achieve a complete shutdown of the three ports, but they were able to keep enough French warships from crossing the Atlantic to give the 1758 expedition against Louisbourg an overwhelming advantage. Only one French squadron, sailing from Brest, made it to Louisbourg. The one from Toulon was kept completely within the Mediterranean, while the one from Rochefort was delayed for a month, which was long enough. Its ships had to turn back to France when they reached Cape Breton waters and spotted a massive British blockade already in place.

The 1758 British expedition against Louisbourg was a combined undertaking, which required amphibious operations and close cooperation between the British Army and the Royal Navy. Placed in command of the land forces was Major-General Jeffery Amherst. It was his first appointment to such a high level. The naval leadership went to Admiral Edward Boscawen, an experienced officer familiar with the waters and weather of Atlantic Canada. Over the course of the campaign, the two men and their officer corps worked together harmoniously, setting a striking example of how a joint command could work.

British warships began to arrive in Halifax in mid-March, joining the ships that had overwintered there. Many more vessels—forming the bulk of the expedition and including transports with thousands of soldiers—reached Halifax in mid-May. A couple weeks were then spent organizing logistics, developing preliminary attack plans, and practicing amphibious landings. This last aspect was crucial, for the British leadership was determined that there would be an attempt to go ashore this time, following the failure of the 1757 expedition. All the officers were also fully aware of what had happened to British Admiral John Byng, who had recently been executed in England for "not having done his utmost" during a campaign in the Mediterranean.

The expedition set sail from Halifax for Louisbourg in late May. In early June, the British armada of roughly 150 vessels, which carried over twenty-seven thousand combatants—sailors as well as soldiers—were stationed off the coast of Louisbourg. The British attacking force contained more than thirteen thousand troops—almost all of them professional British soldiers. The naval support consisted of twenty-three warships with at least fifty guns, and eleven warships with fewer guns. The rest was a host of smaller vessels and transports.

Awaiting them were the defenders of the French colony. The French were in a far stronger position than they had been in back in 1745. They had roughly 3,500 soldiers, militia, Acadian partisans,

This vignette from a larger painting by renowned historical artist Lewis Parker depicts a scene from the 1758 siege. Brigade commander James Wolfe—the man with the telescope—is at Lighthouse Point, watching the bombardment of Louisbourg unfold.

and Aboriginal warriors under the overall command of Governor Augustin de Boschenry de Drucour. Their naval support consisted of six vessels of fifty guns or more, and four vessels with fewer than fifty. The round figure for the French sailors was about five thousand. None of those totals, however, were impressive in comparison with the size of the approaching British force. Moreover, the basic weaknesses of Louisbourg remained. One was that if enemy troops came ashore, they would be able to establish siege batteries on hills overlooking the fortress. Another was that, because of Louisbourg's sailing distance from France or Quebec, the port was vulnerable to blockades that would cut off any hope of supplies or reinforcements.

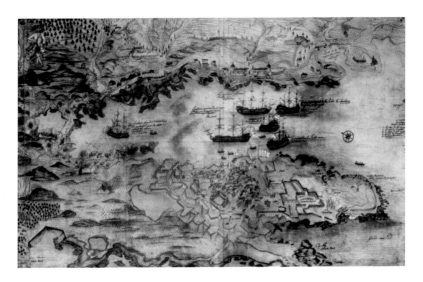

This is a relatively small portion of a huge painting, *Plan du Cap Breton, dit Louisbourg avec ces environs pres (July 26, 1758)*, by an unknown French artist. The full painting attempts to present the complete context and setting of the 1758 siege of Louisbourg. This section highlights the fortified town and shows the largest of the French warships in the harbour.

With the attackers outnumbering the defenders by a ratio of three to one, the odds were definitely in Britain's favour. But what would decide the outcome was whether or not the British could get ashore. If they accomplished that, their superiority in men and materiel would almost certainly prevail.

A British attempt at a landing was delayed several days due to rough seas. Finally, in the early morning hours of June 8, 1758, the attackers tried to come ashore. What happened next, in the confusion of thick smoke, is one of the great dramas in the military history of North America. In the course of a few fortunate moments for the British—and of despair for the French—what seemed like a definite British setback became a success. An amphibious force under the command of Brigadier General James Wolfe gained a

A Confusing Morning That Made History

The British plan of attack on June 8, 1758, called for three separate flotillas of small boats to set out for three separate landing beaches to the south of Louisbourg. Unknown to the French on shore, two of the flotillas were feints. The idea was that the feints would hold the defenders in their two locations so that the *real* landing zone, Anse de la Cormorandière (Kennington Cove), would not be reinforced. Only the flotilla under the command of James Wolfe had orders to attempt a landing.

The French held their fire against Wolfe's contingent until the last moment, and then launched a deadly attack. There was a large loss of British lives and many boats were overturned. Wolfe gave the command to turn around and head back to the troop ships offshore. Yet due to the confusion, and the smoke from all the musket and cannon fire, a few British boats found a spot on the shoreline where the French could not see them. Wolfe noticed what was happening and reversed the orders to turn back around, instead heading for that spot. A relatively small number of British troops climbed up the cliff and surprised the French defenders from an angle they did not expect. Not long after, astonished to see the British ashore, the French commander ordered a retreat. The British were ashore for good. (For a detailed account of this event and the rest of the 1758 siege, see A. J. B. Johnston's *Endgame 1758*.)

foothold ashore at Anse de la Cormorandière (Kennington Cove). It would prove to be a major turning point in the Seven Years' War.

After the landing, the British took their time bringing all their materiel ashore and establishing their camps. With their base secured down the coast from the fortified town, safely beyond French artillery range, the land force under Amherst's command set out to systematically close in on its targets. The first step was to establish major batteries on Lighthouse Point so as to knock out the French position on the Island Battery, and to chase all the French ships into one corner of the harbour. After that, step-by-step, the British would gradually tighten the noose.

After coming ashore, the first goal in Amherst's plan of attack was to establish gun and mortar batteries at Lighthouse Point. They were to knock out the French position on the Island Battery and drive the French warships closer to the town. This engraving illustrates the British as they begin to do just that.

It turned out that the siege took about seven weeks, after which the British brought Louisbourg to the point where virtually all its gun batteries were silenced. British siege positions moved steadily closer to the walls of the town. During the late stages of the attack, civilian areas within the town suffered severely from bombardment, resulting in a high loss of life. On July 22, the King's Bastion Barracks were hit and burned; and a few days later, on July 25, the British captured one of the last two French ships and burned the other.

At last, on July 26—after an eighteen-hour period of profound worry and stress amongst the French leadership and the general community of Louisbourg—the besieged stronghold surrendered. In terms of drama, the story of this capitulation rivals that of the June 8 landing. The next day, July 27, the British marched in and took over Louisbourg.

View from one of the British batteries, showing Louisbourg under attack. The burning French ships in the harbour reveal that this scene was painted near the end of the siege.

Over the next few weeks, the French soldiers and civilian population were placed on ships and transported to France. Not long after, a large contingent of British soldiers sailed to Île Saint-Jean to begin a wholesale removal of every French colonist and Acadian they could round up. The British would continue to garrison Louisbourg for another ten years, until 1768, but providing fewer soldiers as the years passed. Now that the British had Halifax as their major base in the Atlantic region, the former French base had become superfluous to their needs.

In 1760, on orders from Prime Minister William Pitt, the fortifications of Louisbourg were destroyed—just in case a treaty handed Cape Breton back to the French, as it had in 1748. This did not happen. The Treaty of Paris, signed in 1763, confirmed that along the Atlantic coast of North America, France would retain only the archipelago of St.-Pierre et Miquelon. Louisbourg

Despair Within the Town

The July 27, 1758, surrender did not happen quickly or easily. It began at dawn on July 26, with the French assessing the massive damage inflicted on Louisbourg and its fortifications. Under a white flag, they proposed a negotiation of the terms of surrender.

But the British would not negotiate at all. They demanded an unconditional surrender, threatening to launch a total assault on the town otherwise. The French military leadership decided that, for the sake of their honour, they could not submit like that. They decided to make a last stand, and began to prepare. But the civilians saw what was happening and expressed their profound concern. The loss of life by making such a doomed defence would have been horrendous. The French leadership eventually recanted, and accepted the British terms. (For a detailed account of this event and the rest of the 1758 siege, see A. J. B. Johnston's *Endgame 1758*.)

disappeared from the world stage; its period as an overseas imperial dream for France, and a target for New England and Great Britain, was over.

The consequences of what happened at Louisbourg in 1758 were far reaching and long lasting. Not only was it a turning point in the Seven Years' War, it was also a watershed event in the history of Atlantic Canada. When that French stronghold fell, a whole world of relationships and settlements disappeared with it. For the Mi'kmaq and the Maliseet, it was the end of a long era during which they'd had close ties with the French, and the dedicated missionaries provided by them. The capture of Louisbourg, along with the mass removal of thousands of Acadians from throughout the Maritimes, made huge areas of land available for later British settlement. First, in the 1760s, came the New England Planters. Twenty years later, in the aftermath of the American Revolution, came the Loyalists.

Louisbourg did not, however, become a ghost town. The end of the French period was the beginning of a new era. The

This engraving of a painting by British artist Richard Paton aims to depict the events of July 25–26, 1758, when the French ship *Prudent* was set ablaze, and the *Bienfaisant* was captured by the British.

low-lying peninsula where the French population had once been concentrated—the *intra muros* (Latin for "inside the walls") of the once-fortified town—became home to a dozen or so families of Irish, Scottish, and English descent (a few of whom had a direct link to the British capture of the French stronghold in 1758). For well over a century, wooden homes were scattered here and there among the ruins of the bygone French settlement, while an even greater number of families settled along the north side of Louisbourg harbour, higher up the shoreline from the original French fishing properties. A separate community sprang up at Kennington Cove. For decades, the families of nineteenth- and early twentieth-century Louisbourg were left alone to lead their lives where and how they chose.

The town's population was on the upswing, especially after Louisbourg became the winter exportation port for Cape Breton coal. The Sydney & Louisbourg Railway connected the town to

The massive coal pier of late nineteenth-century and early twentieth-century Louisbourg is on the left. In the background is the area known as Havenside. What would later become the Fortress of Louisbourg National Historic Site is not shown in this photo; it is much farther off to the right.

the coalfields and brought in passengers. This era was a definite boom time. By the late nineteenth century, there was a renewed fishery and a blossoming coal export business. An industrial-era infrastructure rose on the north shore of the harbour, where modern Louisbourg had come to be. The new construction included a massive pier. Once again, prosperity was linked to the harbour, as it had been during the French era a century before.

Just as in the original eighteenth-century town, the focal point of reconstructed Louisbourg is the King's Bastion Barracks. Here we see it first under construction in the 1960s, and then completed—the way it looks today.

CHAPTER 6

FROM RUINS TO RECONSTRUCTION

Sir, I am commanded by His Majesty to acquaint you, that...the fortress at Louisbourg...together with all the works and defences of the harbour, be most effectively, and most entirely, demolished. –William Pitt, prime minister of Great Britain, 1760.

What could be more stimulating to the imagination or instructive to the mind...than to look upon a symbolic reconstruction of the Fortress of Louisbourg. –Justice I. C. Rand, Royal Commissioner, 1960.

FOR TWO hundred years, after the British withdrew their last soldiers in 1768, what was left of French colonial Louisbourg lay in ruins. To those few who visited and who knew the history behind the ruins, they served as an evocative reminder of what had once been. People could look at and dig through what was there and take whatever souvenirs they chose. The great nineteenth-century American historian Francis Parkman came to Louisbourg in the late 1800s, leaving behind this romantic description.

> This grassy solitude was once the "Dunkirk of America;" the vaulted caverns where the sheep find shelter from the rain were casemates where terrified women sought refuge from the storms of shot and shell, and the shapeless green mounds were citadel, bastion, rampart and glacis. Here stood Louisbourg; and not all the

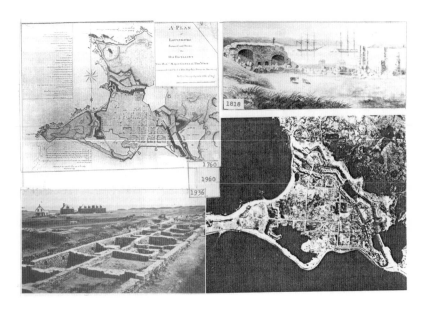

This combination of four images presents scenes from across two centuries. In the upper right is J. E. Woolford's sketch of the ruins of the King's Bastion area in the early 1800s. On the lower left is a photo of ruins of the King's Bastion Barracks, which were stabilized in the 1930s. The Louisbourg Museum is also visible in the background. The two maps show how traces of the fortifications persist long after the actual stone walls and earthen ramparts were blown-up.

efforts of its conquerors, nor all the havoc of succeeding times, have availed to efface it.... The remains of its vast defences still tell their tale of human valor and human woe.

While Parkman seemed happy enough to see Louisbourg as it was—grazing animals, a collection of scattered fences, and a few dozen contemporary wooden houses belonging to families of English or Irish descent—amongst others, the idea gradually began to develop that the vestiges of Louisbourg deserved protection and commemoration of some sort. Individuals and

It was a huge event in 1895 when the General Society of Colonial Wars came up from the United States to raise a memorial marking their ancestors' victory at Louisbourg 150 years earlier. The monument was erected in the King's Bastion area, but it was relocated to Rochefort Point in the 1960s to make way for the reconstruction. It was damaged and shortened in the move.

organizations began pressing for the colourful past of Louisbourg to be marked in ways other than in books and articles.

Louisbourg received its first official commemoration in 1895. This was when the General Society of Colonial Wars from the United States raised a twenty-six-foot-high memorial to the 1745 New England victory and the ensuing loss of life. Some Canadians—notably Acadians and United Empire Loyalist descendants—objected to having an American organization come onto Canadian soil to mark what was a defeat for one half of the country's two founding peoples. When the issue was raised in Parliament, however, the government position was that, because

This is a close-up of the dignitaries involved in the 1926 unveiling of a HSMBC plaque commemorating the historic significance of the King's Bastion at Louisbourg. The cairn and plaque were removed when the reconstruction took place in the 1960s.

it was a private society raising a monument on private land, the raising of the memorial was therefore not any business of the government. And indeed, at the time, the federal government had no policies or regulations about how the country's history should be remembered or marked. It was not until 1919, when an arm's-length advisory body called the Historic Sites and Monuments Board of Canada (HSMBC) was established, that the federal government envisioned it *did* have a role to play in the commemoration of Canadian history. That role was to declare certain persons, places, and events as being of "national significance."

A key player at Louisbourg during this era was retired industrialist-turned-historian Senator J. S. McLennan, who lived near Sydney at an estate called Petersfield. He wrote the first in-depth history of the French regime at Louisbourg—a book first published in 1918, and still in print almost a century later—and lobbied the government to undertake projects to protect the site and tell the story of what happened there. Later, from the 1930s until her death in the 1970s, the senator's daughter, Katharine McLennan, was heavily involved in the development of the Louisbourg site.

During the 1920s, the federal government expropriated all of the private properties on what had been the site of the original French fortified town. Through the HSMBC, the government placed plaques

John Stewart McLennan came to Cape Breton as a manger in the coal industry, and was later appointed to the Senate and became a newspaper publisher. His great passion was history. His classic book *Louisbourg from its Foundation to its Fall*, published in 1918, is still in print.

on stone cairns around the Louisbourg site, designating locations and events of importance. Then in the 1930s, as a make-work project during the Depression, the government oversaw the stabilization of the ruins of the King's Bastion Barracks and Hospital. The culmination of years of effort was the construction of a museum, where artifacts, maps and plans, and other objects of interest would be put on display.

For a generation, the site of the original French Louisbourg stood still, more or less, as a place of ruins with a small museum. Then in 1960, a quite different idea surfaced and quickly took hold. This idea, first supported in connection with putting

The McLennans: Father and Daughter

No family duo played a greater role in the protection of the Louisbourg site than John Stewart McLennan (1853–1939) and his daughter Katharine McLennan (1892–1975). From the late nineteenth century until his death, J. S. McLennan was Louisbourg's most knowledgeable and ardent champion. Katharine took over where he left off, and served as the honorary curator of the museum for thirty years. She made a large model of the French settlement that is still on display. She also looked after the artifact collection and did all she could to preserve and promote the site. She was made a member of the Order of Canada in 1972.

unemployed coal miners to work, was to rebuild a significant portion of the old French town. Senator McLennan had long shown that such an undertaking was possible, thanks to the thousands of detailed documents found in archives in Great Britain and France. What is amazing from the vantage point of the early twenty-first-century, when the emphasis in government is on reducing expenditures, is that the government of the time agreed to take on a project as ambitious and visionary as rebuilding a portion of a long-vanished eighteenth-century town.

This is the official ceremony, held in 1937, to mark the opening of the Louisbourg Museum. Seen here on the steps are Katharine McLennan and Nova Scotia historian and archivist D. C. Harvey. Approaching them with the top hat and walking stick is the Rt. Hon. Lord Tweedsmuir, the Governor General of Canada at the time.

The short explanation is that the political and economic climate in 1960–61 was just right for such a bold idea. There was public interest in heritage matters, a newly elected federal government sympathetic to nation building, and a desperate unemployment problem on Cape Breton Island due to the closures of many mines. Justice I. C. Rand headed up a Royal Commission on the Canadian coal industry, concluding in his report that Cape Breton could benefit from a "symbolic reconstruction" of the once-glorious French fortified town of Louisbourg. Rand said that it would put unemployed coal miners to work, and that, once finished, the rebuilt fortress would attract thousands of tourists to see the results. He didn't make the comparison, but the royal commissioner was undoubtedly thinking Louisbourg could be a sort of "Williamsburg north." Colonial Williamsburg was and still is a major attraction commemorating the colonial era in Virginia.

The Rand Commission's recommendation to rebuild Louisbourg became a reality. In June 1961, the government of the Right Honourable John G. Diefenbaker announced: "The Fortress of Louisbourg is to be restored partially so that future generations can thereby see and understand the role of the Fortress as a hinge of history. The restoration is to be carried out so that the lessons of history can be animated."

There are a couple of ironies worth pointing out. First, it had been British sappers and miners who had systematically blown up Louisbourg's fortifications in 1760, and it was the plight of Cape Breton's miners exactly two hundred years later that provided the impetus for the decision to rebuild the place. Second, it was the relative completeness of Louisbourg's abandonment in the 1750s and 1760s—first by the French, and then a decade later by the British—that eventually allowed the town to rise again. Had Louisbourg been continuously occupied and developed by a large population—as was the case with its contemporary urban centres like Montreal, Quebec, Boston, and New York—the archaeological time capsule that was eighteenth-century Louisbourg would not have been there, waiting for researchers to uncover it, two centuries later.

A second round of connected expropriations took place, enlarging the National Historic Site. This time it was the properties along the north shore—what had come to be called "Old Town"—and down at Kennington Cove. These additional land acquisitions were part of an ambitious new vision of what the Fortress of Louisbourg could be. The thinking at the time called for a large visitors' centre, an administration compound, a bus system to transport visitors, and a buffer zone that had no modern "intrusions," such as houses, churches, or other buildings.

The work of rebuilding Louisbourg did not begin with picks and shovels, backhoes and bulldozers. It began with research and a planning process. From 1961 to 1963, the building trades were put to work erecting an administrative compound a couple of kilometres away from the fortress site and a small housing area on the edge of modern Louisbourg. The latter was where the "project team" moving to the area could live. As for the plans, they needed input not just from architects and engineers, but from historians as well. So the reconstruction phase had to begin in libraries and archives. The original French inhabitants, and the British and New England victors, had left rich treasure troves of records behind in various archives.

This wine glass, manufactured in England between 1710 and 1730, was more intact than most uncovered at Louisbourg. It was found in a barrel-lined well that dates from between 1719 and 1734. Its technical description is: clear glass balustroid stemware with a knopped-stem style.

Newly hired Parks Canada historians located more than five hundred relevant maps and plans, and approximately three-quarters of a million pages of court, parish, and shipping records, as well as property transactions and siege journals. Of course, locating is not the same as understanding. Research and analysis began as quickly as it could. Once the archaeological excavations had commenced, another rich and complementary resource database was brought to bear. Over the years, archaeologists brought

Swivel Gun

One artifact in the Fortress of Louisbourg's archaeological collection, which apparently comes from the early phase of European use of the anchorage at Louisbourg, is a swivel gun. Artillery experts say it dates back to between the 1550s and the late 1600s. It is unknown whether it was thrown overboard on purpose, or by accident during a sea battle, or because it was past usefulness. The artillery piece was found along the north shore of the harbour in the 1840s. One story has it being found in the mud; another has it pulled up by a ship's anchor. The swivel gun was donated to Parks Canada in 1936.

to the light of day several million artifacts the French, British, and New Englanders left behind. The resulting collection is one of the world's largest of the French colonial era.

The amount of historical and archaeological data assembled and studied at Louisbourg was incredible, and it still is, though most of its archives have now been transferred to Cape Breton University. For over half a century now, the historians who toil at and for the Fortress of Louisbourg have generated a sort of "Louisbourg school." Back in 1984, American historian James Axtell wrote that Louisbourg was the most-studied colonial community in North America. Well, an awful lot has been published in the thirty years since then. So too has the archaeological research been celebrated across Canada and abroad. (Artifacts from Louisbourg are often on exhibit in France.) For decades, through its research program, the fortress has been an important contributor to the worldwide study of French colonial life and culture.

This impromptu photo was taken in 1963 to mark the beginning of the reconstruction of Louisbourg after two years of initial, hastily conducted research and design.

To make sense of so much material—documentary, pictorial, and archaeological—the approach at the fortress from the 1960s to the 1990s was, of necessity, an interdisciplinary one. For the first twenty years, teams of archaeologists, historians, engineers, and architects worked together to sort out the evidence building by building and street by street. The reconstruction began in 1963; and when the last of the rebuilt buildings was said to be completed in 1982, roughly fifty structures had been put up, plus a whole lot of fortifications, palisade fences, a quay wall, and small outbuildings. The end result was a remarkable achievement: a full one-fifth of the original town and one quarter of the fortification walls had been restored.

Inside the buildings was another story. Once erected, they needed furnishings. More than eight thousand pieces were

Prime Minister Pierre Trudeau and his new wife Margaret Trudeau (each wearing a white hard hat) visited the fortress during the 1970s. Key Parks Canada personnel were on hand to explain the history and archaeology of the place.

acquired, ranging from tapestries and paintings to wardrobes and desks, from a harpsichord to china and glass. Some, especially in the 1960s, were antiques purchased in France and Quebec. But as time went on, for reasons of cost as well as durability, reproductions of originals came to be preferred.

The buildings and streets provided the setting, but action was needed to truly bring the place and its history to life. People learn in different ways, and several approaches were tried, as they are still. There are exhibits in a variety of indoor settings, and telephones with recorded messages in the King's Bastion. But everyone's favourite way to learn—or so we think—is through interactions with people in costume.

Initially, the period selected as the focus for the reconstruction and furnishing of the fortress was the spring of 1745, just before the bombardment of the first siege. However, once a costumed-animation program was introduced, the date was moved back to 1744, as there was no way to recreate the events of 1745. Throughout the 1970s and 1980s, the idea of visiting Louisbourg during "a moment in time" was the idea that dominated the interpretation, and was a concept the public loved. Of course, the eighteenth-century town wasn't really back.

The Fortress of Louisbourg aims to present a cross-section of eighteenth-century society, from the upper classes to the tradesmen who plied essential crafts.

There are a number of differences between the original town and its reconstruction, beginning with the unseen use of concrete inside various fortification walls and ending with the fact that the late twentieth-century people wearing the clothing of their eighteenth-century namesakes are taller, live longer, and smell better than the original occupants of the place. And then there is the ocean. It, too, is not what it was in 1744.

When Parks Canada archaeologists and engineers tackled the reconstruction of the Louisbourg waterfront in the 1960s they used a large cofferdam to keep the seawater of the harbour at bay. This allowed the archaeologists to investigate the physical remains of the original French infrastructure. They came across the old timbers and stones, and the original iron mooring rings. The odd thing was, the French mooring rings were surprisingly low. They were at or below the water line, depending on high or low tide. What was going on?

The discovery of the submerged mooring rings at the fortress has grown in significance as time goes by. When sea-level data is added, this image is a poster presentation of what's been going on in the land-sea relationship over the past 250 years.

The reason the rings were so low was that there has been two and a half centuries of crustal subsidence and sea level rise. The Geological Survey of Canada has confirmed that high tide at Louisbourg has risen nearly a metre above where it was for the French mariners in the 1700s. Recent analyses by archaeologists and engineers have found that some harbour and nearby coastal locations at Louisbourg have retreated (or been eroded) between fifteen to eighteen metres (nearly sixty feet) over the past 250 years. The more exposed areas, and those with soft sediment, erode faster than areas of hard rock. Looking ahead, the situation is only going to get worse. A body called the Intergovernmental Panel on Climate Change predicts that the next 100 years will likely witness a further 73-centimetre rise in sea level, which is almost equal to the total rise over the past 255 years.

If the sea were always calm, a slowly increasing water level might be a manageable evolution. One could theoretically construct a protective cordon to hold back the gently lapping water. But the North Atlantic is far from always calm. From time to time there are major storm events. The reality at Louisbourg over the past thirty plus years has been that there can be substantial damage during certain storms, especially nor'easters. Significant sections of the shoreline have been eaten away, and elements of

This French plan shows the tidal amplitude on Louisbourg's harbourfront as it was back in the 1740s. What was high tide back then is roughly the low-tide mark today.

the reconstructed Fortress of Louisbourg have been battered and ripped off. There has been great damage to archaeological sites along the exposed shoreline and to barrier beaches. And the frequency and severity of storm events seems to be increasing as time goes by.

Of course, the situation at Louisbourg is far from unique. The Maritimes—and indeed the planet—has many historic sites that, for one reason or another, have been abandoned due to or altered by climate change. Sometimes it's an invasive jungle that has taken over; in other cases, once-thriving centres now lie in deserts that no longer support large-scale societies. Our climate and our world have always been in flux. An example closer to what may be Louisbourg's eventual fate is found in Egypt. What was ancient Alexandria at the time of Queen Cleopatra is now about six metres under water.

So where do those who love Louisbourg go from here? A form of cultural "triage" seems to be the way ahead, one in which a mix of approaches and tools are used. Sometimes a particular site may warrant heroic measures to conserve it; other spots may require rescue archaeology after a storm event. This much is

Coastal Erosion at Louisbourg

During the early stages of the Louisbourg reconstruction project in the 1960s, archaeologists uncovered portions of the original seawall. The wall had been preserved behind mounds of beach sand that accumulated along the shoreline after the abandonment of the fortress in the late eighteenth century. In situ mooring rings projected from the seawall, marking the height of high tide when the wall was constructed in 1743. When geologists from the Geological Survey of Canada compared the mooring ring elevation to current-day tide levels, they recorded an eighty-five-centimetre rise in sea level. This rise has come about for two main reasons: thermal expansion of the oceans, and subsidence. The former is due to warming climate conditions, and the latter is a result of postglacial rebound: now that the weight of the glaciers has lifted, the land is slowly levelling out.

This is one of several instances at Louisbourg where archaeological and geological study have provided evidence of sea level rise, as well as a coastal retreat in the range of fifteen to eighteen metres (fifty to sixty feet) over the past 250 years. To be sure, sea level has been rising and the shores have been retreating for centuries due to postglacial warming conditions. However, it is hard to find physical evidence of this change from periods prior to the twentieth century. The preserved archaeological record at Louisbourg, as well as its historical records, has provided a rare glimpse of coastal change from the mid-eighteenth century until today.

One outcome of this research is an understanding of how the fortress—its fortifications, buildings, gardens, streets, and burial grounds—will be impacted by coastal change in the years to come. The oceans will continue to rise and the shores will continue to shift landward, eventually obliterating the fortress in the decades and centuries ahead. Current conservation efforts prioritize archaeological research to document the coastal heritage before it is lost. There is time to do this now, but the coastal clock is ticking....

–*Rebecca Dunham*

Due to its location, and the way it juts into the Atlantic, the low-lying peninsula at Louisbourg is vulnerable to storms—especially nor'easters.

certain: the challenges of damaging sea surges and ongoing sea rise and subsidence are not going away. Rather, they are going to worsen as time marches on. The peninsula where the heart of French Louisbourg was located is low-lying and mostly flat. Eventually—whether in fifty years, a century, or a millennium—significant portions of the Fortress of Louisbourg reconstruction and its archaeological heritage are not going to be as they are now. Erosion will continue. Some areas will become submerged. The harbour and the ocean that feeds it will win out, as they always have and always will. That day, though on its way, is not here yet. Until it comes, Louisbourg is an unrivalled treasure to be savoured and explored.

ABOUT THE
CONTRIBUTORS

ANNE MARIE LANE JONAH is a Parks Canada historian who has been working at the Fortress of Louisbourg National Historic Site of Canada since 2003. She has authored numerous articles and conference papers on the French colonial period and recently co-authored *French Taste in Atlantic Canada*, published by Cape Breton University Press in 2012.

REBECCA DUNHAM is a Parks Canada archaeologist with extensive experience in the research and management of cultural resources. Since the 1990s she has worked mostly at the Fortress of Louisbourg, but has also spent time overseeing projects out of the Atlantic Service Centre in Halifax, Nova Scotia. She is the author of many papers and reports.

SELECTED BIBLIOGRAPHY

WEBSITES

"At the Table." CBC Maritimes interview with John Johnston: cbc.ca/atthetable/2012/11/john-johnston.html

Fortress of Louisbourg Association: fortressoflouisbourg.ca

Fortress Research Site: fortress.cbu.ca/default.htm

Parks Canada: pc.gc.ca/eng/lhn-nhs/ns/louisbourg/index.aspx

"Saving Louisbourg." CBC Land and Sea. Broadcast on October 14, 2012. Contains interviews with Anne Marie Lane Jonah, Rebecca Duggan, A. J. B. Johnston, and Lester Marchand: cbc.ca/landand-sea/2012/10/saving-louisbourg.html

BOOKS

Balcom, B. A. *The Cod Fishery of Isle Royale, 1713–1758.* Ottawa: Parks Canada, 1984.
———. "Honour and Fate: *La Renommée* and the Defence of Louisbourg, 1745," vol. 24/25, no. 1, Spring/Summer, *The Nashwaak Review*, 2010.
———. "Defending Unama'ki: Mi'kmaw Resistance in Cape Breton, 1745," vol. 22/23, no. 1, Spring/Summer, *The Nashwaak Review*, 2009.
———. "For King and Profit: Louisbourg Privateers." Ed: Yves Tremblay. *Canadian Military History Since the 17th Century. Proceedings of the Canadian Military History Conference* (Ottawa: May 5–9, 2000). Ottawa: National Defence, 2001.
Balcom, B. A., and A. J. B. Johnston. "Missions to the Mi'kmaq: Malagawatch and Chapel Island in the 18th Century," vol. 9, *Journal of the Royal Nova Scotia Historical Society*, 2006. 115–40.

Donovan, Ken. "'After Midnight We Danced Until Daylight': Music, Song and Dance in Cape Breton, 1713–1758," vol. XXXII, no. 1 (Autumn), *Acadiensis*, 2002. 3–28.

———. "Communities and Families: Family Life and Living Conditions in Eighteenth-Century Louisbourg." Ed. Eric Krause et al. *Aspects of Louisbourg: Essays on the History of an 18th-Century French Community.* 1995. 117–49.

———. "Imposing Discipline Upon Nature: Gardens, Agriculture and Animal Husbandry in Cape Breton, 1713–1758," no. 64 (Fall), *Material Culture Review*, 2006. 20–37.

———. "The Marquis de Chabert and the Louisbourg Observatory in the 1750s" vol. XLIV, no. 3 (Summer), *American Neptune*, 1984. 186–97.

———. "Slaves in Île Royale, 1713–1758," vol. 5, *French Colonial History*, 2004. 25–42.

Duggan, Rebecca. "Skeletons in the Cellar." Eds. Paul Erickson and Jonathan Fowler. *Underground Nova Scotia: Stories of Archaeology.* Halifax: Nimbus Publishing, 2010.

Fry, Bruce W., *'An Appearance of Strength': The Fortifications of Louisbourg*, 2 vols. Ottawa: Parks Canada, 1984.

Johnston, A .J. B. *Control and Order: The Evolution of French Colonial Louisbourg, 1713–1758.* East Lansing, MI: Michigan State University Press, 2001.

———. *Endgame 1758: The Promise, the Glory and the Despair of Louisbourg's Last Decade.* Sydney, NS: Cape Breton University Press, 2007.

———. "Land & Sea & Louisbourg: 5000 Years and Counting," vol. 26/27, no. 1 (Summer/Fall), *The Nashwaak Review*, 2011.

———. *Life and Religion at Louisbourg, 1713–1758.* Montreal: McGill-Queen's University Press, 1996.

———. *Storied Shores: St. Peter's, Isle Madame and Chapel Island in the 17th and 18th Centuries.* Sydney, NS: Cape Breton University Press, 2004.

Krause, Eric, Carol Corbin Krause, and William O'Shea, eds. *Aspects of Louisbourg: Essays on the History of an Eighteenth-Century French Community in North America Published to Commemorate the 275th Anniversary of the Founding of Louisbourg.* Sydney: University College of Cape Breton Press, 1995.

Jonah, Anne Marie Lane, and Chantal Véchambre. *French Taste in Atlantic Canada—1604–1758: A Gastronomic History.* Sydney: Cape Breton University Press, 2012.

Jonah, Anne Marie Lane, "Small Pleasures: Gifts and Trade in Personal Correspondence between France and Louisbourg," vol. 14, *Journal of the Royal Nova Scotia Historical Society*. Halifax: RNSHS, 2011.

———. "Unequal Transitions: Two Métis Women in Eighteenth-Century Louisbourg," vol. 11, *French Colonial History*. East Lansing: Michigan State University Press, 2010.

———. "A Necessary Luxury: Chocolate in Louisbourg and New France," ed. Louis E. Grivetti and Howard-Yana Shapiro. *Chocolate: History Culture and Heritage, an Anthology of Historical Essays*. New Jersey: Wiley and Sons, 2009.

McLennan, J. S. *Louisbourg: From its Foundation to its Fall*. 1918. Reprint, Halifax: Nimbus Publishing, 2011.

Moore, Christopher. *Louisbourg Portraits*. Toronto: Macmillan, 1982.

Rawlyk, George A. *Yankees at Louisbourg*. Orono: University of Maine, 1967.

Sawlor, Elaine. *Beyond the Fog: Louisbourg After the Final Siege, 1758–1968*. Sydney: City Printers, 2008.

IMAGE CREDITS

We want to acknowledge and express our special gratitude to the following Parks Canada staff for their assistance in locating and providing scans of most of the images featured in this book: Ken Donovan, Rebecca Dunham, David Ebert, Ruby Fougère, Heather Gillis, Maria O'Hearn, Heidi Moses, and Adam Young of the Fortress of Louisbourg National Historic Site of Canada; Theresa Bunbury, Lillian Stewart, Miriam Walls, and Carla Wheaton of the Mainland Nova Scotia Field Unit and Charles Burke and Guy LeBlanc of the National Office, Halifax branch. Other images came courtesy of: John Shaw and Bob Taylor of the Geological Survey of Canada; Archives nationales de France; Beaton Institute of Cape Breton University (thanks to Jane Arnold and Catherine Arseneau); Bibliothèque nationale de France; the Library of Congress; the estate of the late Lewis Parker; and the Nova Scotia Museum.

All photos courtesy of Parks Canada, Fortress of Louisbourg National Historic Site with the exception of the following.

Archives Nationales d' outre mar (10, 14, 25, 43[l], 46, 74, 111); Courtesy of Archives nationales de France Marine (82, 84); Bellin, *Le petit atlas maritime* (16); Biblioteque Nationale de France (8, 58); Courtesy of Chicago Library (28); Andre Cornellier (50[b]); Duhamel Du Monceau, *Traité général des pesches* (66); Geological Society of Canada (4); Heidi Moses (32, 105); Horst Paufler (50[t]); James McConnell Library, Cape Breton Regional Library (101); Len Wagg, Communications Nova Scotia (3, 68); Courtesy of the estate of Lewis Parker and Cape Breton University (44, 88); Library of Congress, Washington, DC (89); Marguerite-Bourgeoys Museum (43[r]); Ministère de la Défence, Service Historique de l'Armée de Terre (37); Nova Scotia Museum (22, 72); Nova Scotia Archives (71); National Archives of Canada (19); Provenence unknown (69, 92); Public domain (13, 21, 86); Perry Jackson, *Saltscapes* (32, 54, 64, 109, 113); Raytel Photo (102[r]); Rebecca Dunham (5); William L. Clements Library, University of Michigan (80); Yvon LeBlanc (23).

INDEX

Numbers set in italics refer to images